The Trompe L'Oeil Effect

B.J. IRONS

Copyright © B.J. Irons 2024.

B.J. Irons asserts the moral right to be identified as the author of this work.

Artwork: Adobe Stock - © Yuliya Kirayonak, kichigin19.
Cover designed by Spectrum Books.

Print ISBN: 978-1-915905-52-9

All rights reserved. No part of this text may be reproduced, transmitted, downloaded, decompiled, reverse engineered or stored in or introduced into any information storage and retrieval system, in any form or by any means without the express written permission of the author or Spectrum Books, except for brief quotations used for promotion or in reviews.

This book is entirely a work of fiction. The names, characters and incidents portrayed in it are the work of the author's imagination. Any resemblance to actual persons, living or dead, or events is entirely coincidental.

First edition, Spectrum Books, 2024.

Discover more LGBTQ+ books at www.spectrum-books.com

Other Titles by B.J. Irons

Stand-Alone Titles

The Cul-de-Sac

Rippling Waters

Sinfluenced

The Gift That Keeps on Taking

The Fire Island Ice Queen

Second-Guess

Master of the Bluffs

Up Your HOA Hole

Rest Ashored: Rehomo Beach

The Greek Mythologay Series

Meduso: Book 1

Arrogance: Book 2

Orpheus: Book 3

Hermes: Book 4

Hephaestus: Book 5

The Bosses of Bane Series

The Onyx Demon: Book 1

Trompe L'Oeil :

An artistic technique that uses realistic imagery to create the optical illusion that depicted objects exist in three dimensions. The phrase is French for "deceive the eye," and this style often tricks viewers into perceiving painted details—such as objects, architectural elements, or textures—as if they were real and physically present. Trompe L'Oeil is commonly used in murals, ceilings, or decorative artworks to give the illusion of depth, space, or tangible objects where none actually exist.

Chapter 1

Gavin loosened his tie, the fantastic night air a welcome relief after a long day, as he strolled down the neon-lit streets of the city. The steady hum of life pulsed around him, a cacophony of car horns, muffled conversations, and the faint strains of music spilling out from bars and late-night cafés. Towering skyscrapers glistened above, their windows reflecting the vibrant glow of billboards and streetlamps. The scent of grilled street food mingled with the sharpness of gasoline and distant cigarette and marijuana smoke, creating an intoxicating blend that clung to the air.

As he walked, the city gradually began to thin out. The streets were less crowded and quieter, with only the occasional pedestrian and cyclist passing by. The buildings lowered in stature, giving way to trees, their shadows long and soft under the golden glow of the lampposts. Gavin turned off the main avenue into a narrow path leading toward the park—a still refuge from the city's endless motion.

The park was an entirely different world, a quiet, secluded oasis. The lights from the city faded into the distance, replaced by the soft glow of the few remaining lampposts that lined the path. It was mostly dark here, the thick canopy of trees filtering what little moonlight could reach the ground. The air smelled different, too—earthy, cool, with a hint of damp grass and fallen leaves.

Gavin moved through the park, the sound of his leather shoes tapping softly on the gravel path, a steady rhythm in the stillness. A dark, wooden pavilion came into view ahead, its silhouette stark against the night. The structure was simple, just a roof held up by wooden columns and beams with picnic tables arranged neatly underneath. Further back, a restroom stood—an old stone structure that looked as if it hadn't seen much use in recent months. Still, there was not a soul in sight.

It was quiet. Too quiet.

Gavin slowed his pace as he neared the pavilion, something prickling at the edge of his senses. He scanned the area, his sharp eyes catching the empty tables, the vacant benches, and the gentle rustling of the trees that seemed to close in around him. Gavin wasn't alone. He could feel it.

Just as he stepped into the pavilion, a noise came from behind. Gavin knew someone had followed him.

"Can I help you?" Gavin's tone was calm, almost bored, as he turned around.

His eyes fell on a figure shadowed by the night, stepping out from the line of trees. The man's posture was casual, but there was something predatory in his movement—deliberate, calculated.

"Really?" The stranger's voice was soft but laced with amusement. "You're going to pretend you don't know who I am?"

Gavin felt the corner of his mouth twitch upward in a smirk. His eyes narrowed as he tilted his head slightly, hands slipping casually into his pockets.

"You tell me," he said with a sly shrug.

The man stepped closer into the pavilion's dim light, revealing sharp features framed by dark hair. His expression was unreadable, but his eyes locked onto Gavin's with a burning intensity.

Gavin didn't flinch, didn't step back. Instead, he watched, intrigued, as the man closed the distance between them. Then, in one smooth motion, the man leaned in, his voice barely above a whisper as his breath brushed Gavin's ear.

"Let me remind you, then," the man seductively whispered, his tone dripping with something between malice and anticipation.

Gavin held his ground, but his heart beat a little faster.

The game had begun.

The man firmly gripped his hands onto Gavin's hips, pushing him to the nearest wooden column to balance themselves as the man thrust his body into Gavin's. His lips pressed into Gavin's with practiced ease.

Gavin couldn't help but close his eyes. Every muscle in his body relaxed as he gave in to this sexy man who was up against him.

"We shouldn't be doing this," Gavin protested, even as he found himself melting into the stranger's embrace.

"But you want to," the man murmured, his lips moving to Gavin's neck. "I can feel it. You're hot for me, Gavin. You always have been. And I'm going to make you fucking scream with pleasure."

Gavin moaned as the man's hands roamed over his body, caressing his chest and abdomen. He felt his cock hardening in his pants, straining against the fabric as the stranger's lips found him again.

Of course, Gavin knew who this man was. His name was Colton, and their one-time sexual fling months ago had now been a weekly occurrence.

Colton's tongue explored Gavin's mouth, tasting and teasing. Gavin responded eagerly, their tongues twisting and dancing together.

"Let's move to the picnic table," Colton sensually whispered, his breath hot against Gavin's ear. "I want to taste every inch of your body."

Gavin soon followed him to the wooden picnic table, his heart pounding with anticipation. Colton pushed him down onto the table before ripping off Gavin's clothes savagely. His hands soon took a mind of their own and roamed over Gavin's chest and stomach.

"You're so fucking hot," Colton seductively whispered, his lips moving to Gavin's nipples. He sucked and bit hard, making Gavin gasp with pleasure.

Colton's hands then moved to Gavin's pants, tugging them

down to reveal his hard cock. He pulled Gavin's underwear band down and then stroked and squeezed the exposed shaft, making Gavin moan with pleasure.

"You like that?" Colton asked, his voice husky with desire. "You like it when I touch you?"

"Yes," Gavin gasped, his hips thrusting up to meet Colton's hand. "Fuck, yes."

Colton soon bent down and took Gavin's cock into his mouth, sucking and licking at the sensitive head. Gavin cried out with pleasure, his hands clutching at Colton's thick, jet-black hair.

As Colton continued to devour Gavin's cock, his fingers found Gavin's hole beneath his underwear, teasing and probing at the tight ring of muscle. Gavin instantly moaned as Colton pushed his finger inside him, the sensation both slightly painful and incredibly arousing.

"I want to fuck you here and now, in public," Colton growled, his lips moving to Gavin's ear. "I want to feel your tight hole around my dick."

Gavin nodded, unable to speak. He wanted it, too; he wanted to feel Colton's stiff and aching cock deep inside him.

Colton retrieved a small pack of lube from his pocket, ripped it open, and slathered the contents on his cock and then Gavin's hole through his underwear.

In one quick, smooth motion, Colton rose to his feet and aggressively spun Gavin around. One hand gripped Gavin's neck, and the other firmly grasped his hips, forcing him to bend over the picnic table.

The only thing between Colton and Gavin's smooth ass was Gavin's underwear, still not fully pulled down. Colton tugged at the center to show his aggression and ripped them apart with all his might.

Gavin couldn't help but yelp at the sound of his underwear being torn apart. It was both startling and sexy as hell.

It didn't take long for Colton to position his throbbing

cock so that it was directly aligned with Gavin's eager hole. Colton pushed inside slowly, letting Gavin adjust to the size and sensation.

"Oh fuck!" Gavin moaned, his hands clutching at the edge of the table. "Yes, fuck me. Harder."

Colton obliged, fucking Gavin with long, deep strokes. Gavin cried out with pleasure, his hips bucking up to meet Colton's thrusts.

"You feel so damn good," Colton gasped, his hands tightening their grip on Gavin's hips. "So fucking tight."

Gavin whimpered, his own cock throbbing with pleasure as he reached to stroke it vigorously. He could feel his orgasm building, the sensation intense and overwhelming.

"I'm going to cum," Gavin gasped, his hips grinding wildly against Colton. "Oh fuck, I'm going to cum."

Colton slammed into Gavin with the greatest intensity a few final times, then stilled as he came, filling Gavin's hole with his hot seed. Gavin cried out, his own orgasm crashing over him like a wave.

They lay there, panting and spent. Gavin felt a twinge of guilt, but he pushed it aside. It had been amazing, just as it always had with Colton.

As Colton pulled up his pants, he studied Gavin closely as Gavin re-clothed himself. "You have the best fucking ass in town," Colton shared.

Gavin couldn't help but turn red before chuckling, choosing to ignore Colton's compliment by changing the subject altogether. "I still can't believe you dragged me out here."

"Hey. Don't blame me. I can tell you wanted it. You might have been hesitant at first, but I knew there was no way you could resist," Colton shared.

Gavin raised his brow. "Resist what? You? Or the thrill of being in public?"

"Both, plus my dick, of course," Colton said while offering a sly smirk.

It was that look that made Colton so irresistible to Gavin. That slick smile with those bright white teeth. Gavin knew Colton was that bad boy he had always dreamed about in his fantasies. Never did he imagine these fantasies would eventually become a weekly reality for him.

"Whatever helps you sleep at night," Gavin coolly responded.

Suddenly, Gavin felt Colton's body hug him from behind. Colton's lips trailed and nibbled on Gavin's neck while Gavin finished buttoning up his shirt.

"You next to me in bed with my dick permanently in your ass all night would definitely help me sleep," Colton shared.

Gavin couldn't help but roll his eyes and then push himself away from Colton's grasp. "You know that's not possible. I don't know why you'd even suggest it."

"A guy can dream," Colton added.

All Gavin could do was shrug. "Well, I guess I better get going. Text me later?"

"You betcha," Colton stated before lunging forward to plant one more kiss on Gavin, hoping to let it linger until their next sexual rendezvous.

"Bye," Gavin simply stated as he departed, still afraid to offer any sentimental comments to Colton. For Gavin, this was strictly lust. Although his encounters with Colton had been going on for months now and were beyond passionate, that was all he wanted to offer Colton. There was nothing more to it. This was a no-strings-attached relationship, although Gavin sensed Colton was starting to desire more.

The cool night air clung to Gavin's skin as he left the park, his thoughts still swirling from his encounter with Colton. His heart raced, though the park had already faded into the distance behind him. The city loomed ahead once more, its lights and sounds filling the night as if nothing had changed. But for Gavin, everything had. His body surged with a restless energy, a mix of elation and guilt, two forces constantly at odds within him.

The streets were alive, buzzing with the usual chaos of nightlife. Neon signs flickered over storefronts, the whirr of car engines and voices merging into a chorus of urban noise. The scent of fried food, spilled beer, and exhaust filled the air, overwhelming his senses as he moved through the familiar maze of the city. His pace quickened as he passed crowds of strangers who were too engrossed in their own lives to notice him. They never did. His sleek, dark suit and polished shoes blended seamlessly into the nighttime flow, another anonymous figure drifting through the heart of the city.

After what felt like hours, Gavin finally reached his building. He punched in the code at the door, the quiet beep unlocking the entrance, and made his way inside. The lobby was dimly lit and empty, just as Gavin preferred. The walk to his luxury apartment was silent, offering him a moment of stillness as he drifted down the hall.

When Gavin reached his door, he entered his home, greeted by the familiar warmth of his space. The soft lighting and the elegant décor, all carefully chosen, welcomed him like an old friend. He moved through the open-plan living area and into the master bedroom, his body yearning for rest yet reluctant to stop moving. He tugged at the collar of his button-down shirt as he stepped into the room, unbuttoning it slowly, savoring the sensation of the brisk air touching his bare chest as he let the fabric fall to the floor.

His leather shoes were next, slipping off with ease, followed by his slacks, which he tossed onto the bed. The room was a reflection of his carefully curated life—clean lines, neutral tones, everything in its place. But tonight, it felt hollow.

He crossed into the adjoining bathroom. The space was pristine, gleaming under the warm overhead lights. The marble countertops were spotless, a bright white sink set into the cool surface, and the large mirror stretched across the wall. Gavin caught his reflection and stood still, examining himself. His skin had a glow to it, flushed with the thrill of the night, a sheen of sweat from his earlier tryst still clinging to his body. His dark hair was slightly tousled, eyes bright, and lips slightly swollen from kisses. He looked… *alive*.

He smiled at his reflection, proud of the way he looked. He embraced the glow of his skin and the way his body seemed more defined and vital. But as he caught sight of the torn fabric of his underwear—a huge rip along the back-middle crease, a reminder of his reckless encounter—his smile faded. Gavin slipped them off, discarding the ruined pair in the back of his closet, and pulled on a fresh pair of black boxer briefs. The soft fabric clung to his hips as he padded back into the bedroom, the cool sheets calling him.

He slid into bed, the chilliness of the linen comforting against his heated skin. His head sank into the pillow, and for a moment, a deep sense of satisfaction washed over him. His body relaxed, finally at ease, and a small smile tugged at the corner of his mouth. He had indulged himself, taken what he wanted, and allowed himself to feel victorious.

But then his eyes drifted to the photo on his nightstand, a simple frame containing the image of his husband and their son. His husband's warm smile, his son's innocent grin—they stared back at him, a stark reminder of the life he had built, the life he was risking by continuing to meet with Colton.

Gavin's stomach tightened, the elation draining from his body as guilt flooded in. The affair had been going on for months now, and each time, he told himself it would be the last.

Each time, the lie grew heavier, the guilt deeper. He had everything—a loving husband, a beautiful son, a life people would envy—and yet, here he was, betraying it all. He stared at the photo a little longer, his heart aching with regret. But even as the guilt gnawed at him, exhaustion pulled him under. His eyes grew heavy, and despite the turmoil in his chest, sleep claimed him. The smile he had worn earlier was long gone, replaced by a deep, unsettling weight that followed him into his dreams.

Chapter 2

Gavin awoke slowly, his body shifting under the navy satin sheets as the soft morning light filtered through the partially drawn curtains. He flipped over in bed, instinctively reaching for the warm body that should have been beside him. But the space was empty. His hand met only the cold, crumpled sheets.

His husband, Eric, must have left early again. The hospital, of course—early morning procedures, surgeries, rounds. It seemed like it was becoming a daily routine. Gavin stared at the empty side of the bed, his irritation bubbling to the surface. Not even a kiss goodbye. Not even a gentle nudge to wake him.

Just... gone.

He sighed deeply, running a hand through his disheveled hair. It felt like a pattern now, a growing chasm between them. There was once a time when Eric never left without a word or a touch to remind Gavin he was still loved and cared for. But now, it seemed like that warmth was slipping away, lost in the hustle of work and routine. Gavin closed his eyes, willing away the frustration, before finally throwing back the covers.

Dragging himself out of bed, he moved to his ensuite bathroom, his mind already shifting to the day ahead. After a long, hot shower that left his skin tingling, Gavin dressed, slipping into one of his favorite suits. It was a charcoal gray masterpiece of Italian design, custom-tailored to fit him perfectly. The fabric was soft, lightweight, yet structured—designed to flatter his athletic frame. The lapels were thin, the stitching invisible, and the inside was lined with silk, embossed with his initials. He pulled on a crisp white dress shirt, buttoning it carefully, before slipping on a dark silk tie and a pair of polished black leather shoes. Every detail, from the cufflinks to the tie bar, spoke of wealth, power, and meticulous taste—the hallmark of a successful real estate agent who commanded respect.

Satisfied with his appearance, Gavin made his way into the kitchen. The space was immaculate, gleaming with sleek, white cabinetry that stretched from floor to ceiling. The countertops were a smooth, cool marble, reflecting the overhead lighting, while a large kitchen island dominated the center of the room. Its surface was pristine, save for a neatly arranged bowl of fresh fruit and a vase of white lilies that stood as a decorative centerpiece. The chrome appliances were state-of-the-art, with a built-in espresso machine that thrummed softly as it brewed his morning coffee.

Gavin moved about the kitchen with ease, the scent of freshly ground beans filling the air as the espresso machine worked its magic. He grabbed a white ceramic mug from the cabinet, its subtle weight familiar in his hand. The rich, dark liquid streamed into the cup, its surface smooth, releasing a heady aroma that stirred his senses. He lifted the cup to his lips, the first sip warming him from the inside out, bittersweet and bold. He let the taste linger on his tongue before placing the cup on the marble countertop.

Pacing the length of the kitchen, Gavin's eyes landed on the fridge. Family photos were stuck to it with colorful magnets—scenes of happiness and love. In one picture, Eric was dressed in his neon green swim trunks, his arm around Gavin's waist, both of them smiling widely in front of a beach sunset. Another was of their son, Ashton, just eight years old, grinning brightly as he held up a fishing pole from their summer vacation last year. Ashton was the spitting image of Eric, with his messy light brown hair and bright, inquisitive eyes. Another photo showed the three of them, hands linked, walking down a tree-lined path during the fall, leaves crunching underfoot.

His gaze drifted to the hallway just beyond the kitchen, where framed family portraits hung on the wall. One showed Ashton dressed for his school recital, and another showed him riding his bike for the first time, his face filled with excitement. In all of them, they looked perfect, like the family every couple dreamed of having—happy, fulfilled, secure.

Gavin paused, the weight of the photos pressing down on him. He couldn't ask for a better life, could he? A loving husband, a bright and beautiful son, a successful career, and a home straight out of a luxury magazine. Yet, despite all this, he was risking it—jeopardizing everything he had worked for.

The thought of Colton crept back into his mind, unbidden but irresistible. His breath hitched slightly as memories of last night in the park flashed across his consciousness—the heat, the thrill, the adrenaline rush that had carried him through the night. It felt like an addiction now, a dangerous secret he couldn't seem to stop indulging. And now, standing in his perfect kitchen, looking at his perfect family, the guilt ate away at him, bitter and sharp.

He took another sip of his coffee, the warmth doing little to soothe the unease that settled in his chest. Setting the mug down in the sink, Gavin exhaled long and slow before heading to his bedroom. He needed to grab his laptop bag before heading out to the office.

The master bedroom was just as pristine as it had been this morning; the bed was made perfectly, with the sheets tucked tight. His bag sat neatly in the corner, ready for another day of high-stakes deals and fast-paced meetings. Gavin slung it over his shoulder, his mind still haunted by the faces in the photos, the people he loved, but somehow, he couldn't stop hurting.

As he walked out the door, locking it behind him, the weight of his double life settled heavily on his shoulders.

He was a man who seemed to have it all, but beneath the surface, everything was teetering on the edge. And today, as he made his way into the world, the shame followed him, a shadow he couldn't shake.

Gavin made the city walk down the hustle and bustle of streets and sidewalks until he arrived just outside his real estate office. The sun was already high, glinting off the glass windows of the towering buildings, casting reflections down onto the sidewalks below. The city was alive, people hurrying to and fro, phones pressed to their ears, briefcases swinging as they rushed into their respective offices. Gavin paused, hand resting on the door handle, taking in the familiar energy of the day, ready to step into the building, away from the crisp morning air.

As he straightened his suit jacket, something caught his eye—a small, tattered cart set up just across the street, a sight so out of place amidst the gleaming storefronts and high-end cafés. Gavin recognized the vendor immediately. He had seen the man there before, selling trinkets and knick-knacks, just trying to scrape by while living in the shadow of the towering wealth around him. Today, the vendor's cart was loaded with a new set of items—small, colorful stuffed animals arranged in neat rows. They were Hunchkins, the latest craze sweeping through the city, a combination of cute and quirky farm animals that had every child clamoring to collect them.

Hunchkins were tiny, almost pocket-sized, with soft, plush bodies and exaggerated features. Each one was a blend of farm animals, mixing bright, imaginative colors with odd combinations. Some had the body of a pig but the ears and spots of a cow, while others were sheep with duck feet or chickens with horse tails. They were weird, adorable, and absurdly popular with kids. Gavin knew Ashton would love one of them—he had been begging for a new Hunchkin for weeks now.

Gavin crossed the street, his eyes locking on one Hunchkin in particular. It sat in the middle of the vendor's display, perched atop the others, with its bright turquoise body standing out against the sea of pastels. The creature had the long ears of a rabbit but the plump body and curly tail of a pig, its little snout speckled with bright pink freckles. It wore a miniature yellow bandana around its neck, and its wide, round eyes seemed to sparkle in the morning light.

"How much for that one?" Gavin asked, pointing to the turquoise Hunchkin.

The vendor, an older man with sun-worn skin and graying hair peeking out from under a faded cap, looked up from behind the cart. He smiled warmly, recognizing Gavin from his previous visits to the area.

"Ah, Mr. Gavin!" the vendor exclaimed, his voice thick with a foreign accent. "That one, the little pig-rabbit? Oh, it's a good choice! Very popular with the children."

Gavin smiled, nodding slightly. "Yes, my son, Ashton, will love it. So, how much?"

The vendor rubbed his hands together, glancing at the stuffed animal before meeting Gavin's eyes. "For you, Mr. Gavin, twenty dollars."

Gavin raised an eyebrow, feeling the weight of his wallet in his pocket. "Twenty? For just one of these?" He looked at the Hunchkin again, the price seeming steep for a small toy.

The vendor's smile faded slightly, his tone becoming more serious. "They're hard to get now, you know? Everyone wants them, but there are only so many. The price, it's what the market is, Mr. Gavin."

Gavin considered this for a moment, glancing down at the vendor's cart at the man who was clearly struggling to make ends meet. He felt a twinge of guilt, knowing that twenty dollars was nothing more than pocket change for him, but for this man, it likely made a significant difference.

Without another word, Gavin reached into his wallet

and pulled out a crisp fifty-dollar bill, handing it over to the vendor. "Here. Take fifty and keep the change."

The vendor's eyes widened, and he seemed taken aback. "Fifty? No, no, Mr. Gavin, that's too much! I can't—"

Gavin waved him off, shaking his head. "No, really. Keep it. It's fine."

The vendor hesitated, his hand shaking slightly as he took the bill. "You are too kind, Mr. Gavin. Thank you, thank you so much." He clutched the fifty tightly, his eyes filled with genuine gratitude. "Your son, he will love this Hunchkin, I promise."

Gavin nodded, his expression softening. "I'm sure he will." He reached down, gently taking the turquoise Hunchkin from the cart and cradling it in his hand. The fabric was soft beneath his fingers, the little creature's eyes staring up at him as if it were alive.

As he turned to walk away, heading back toward the towering office building, Gavin couldn't help but glance over his shoulder one last time at the vendor. The man was still standing there, watching him go, the fifty-dollar bill clenched securely in his hand.

With the Hunchkin in his grasp, Gavin made his way to the entrance of his office building. The glossy glass doors loomed ahead, the busy street behind him reflected in the lustrous surface. He took a deep breath, preparing for another day of negotiations and high-stakes deals, but something felt off. A strange sensation crawled up the back of his neck as his hand touched the door handle of the office building.

He stopped, turning slowly to look around. The street was as busy as ever, people moving in every direction, faces blurred in the rush of the city. Yet, there was an odd stillness to it all, as if time had slowed. Gavin scanned the crowd, his eyes darting from person to person, searching for something—*someone*—out of place.

A flicker of movement caught his eye, far down the street,

near a row of parked cars and yellow taxis. Someone stood there, partially obscured by a lamppost, their posture rigid, as if they were frozen in place. For a split second, Gavin thought he saw the glint of something metallic—a camera lens, perhaps—pointed directly at him.

His heart skipped a beat, the feeling of being watched creeping over him like a cold shadow. He took a step back, his grip tightening around the stuffed animal in his hand, eyes narrowing as he tried to get a better look. But whoever it was had already vanished into the crowd, disappearing as quickly as they had appeared.

Gavin shook his head, brushing off the strange feeling. He was being paranoid, surely. It was just another busy day in the city. But as he stepped into the building, the cool, sterile air of the lobby washing over him, that restless feeling lingered. Little did Gavin know, his instincts were right—someone had been watching, and they had captured his every move.

Chapter 3

Gavin strode through the towering glass doors of his real estate office building, the scent of polished floors and fresh coffee greeting him as he entered. The gleaming, modern design of the lobby mirrored the bustling energy of the high-stakes world he navigated daily. His trendy shoes clicked softly against the marble tiles as he made his way toward the elevators, his mind already shifting to the day's tasks.

But as he passed the front desk, the familiar voice of Amanda, the front desk assistant, stopped him in his tracks. "Good morning, Gavin!" she called, her bright smile lighting up her face. "Spencer would like a word with you."

Gavin raised an eyebrow, slowing his pace as he turned to face her. "Spencer?" His curiosity was piqued. Rarely did Gavin's boss call impromptu meetings. "Did he mention what it's about?"

Amanda shook her head, her perfectly styled hair bouncing with the movement. "No, just that he'd like to see you when you have a minute. I think he's in his office now."

Gavin offered a polite nod. "Thanks, Amanda. I'll head there now."

As he made his way toward Spencer's office, Gavin's mind wandered about the meaning behind this sudden summoning. Hopefully, it was nothing too bad. Sure, they were friends outside of work—often sharing drinks after closing a big deal or hitting the golf course on weekends—but Spencer wasn't the type to mix business with pleasure. If he wanted a chat, it had to be important.

He arrived at Spencer's door, which was ajar, revealing the meticulously designed interior of his boss' office. Gavin knocked lightly on the doorframe, his eyes immediately falling on Spencer, who was mid-conversation on his phone. Spencer, always well put together, was leaning back in his high-backed leather chair, his legs crossed casually. His blonde hair was perfectly styled, not a strand out of place, and his designer suit—a crisp gray number with subtle pinstripes—fit him like a glove. Even over the phone, his charisma radiated; his sharp features softened slightly as he waved Gavin inside, motioning for him to sit down.

Gavin stepped into the office, taking a seat in one of the plush leather chairs that faced Spencer's imposing mahogany desk. The office itself was a blend of sophistication and modern style. Dark wood panels lined the walls, shelves neatly adorned with real estate awards, framed magazine covers, and a few personal photos. One wall was dominated by floor-to-ceiling windows, offering a sweeping view of the city skyline. A glass coffee table, strategically placed in front of the guest chairs, held a few artfully placed magazines and a single orchid in a delicate vase. The whole room exuded success.

Spencer's voice softened as he finished his call. "Alright, let's touch base on that later. I have someone in my office now. Talk soon." He hung up the phone, his smile widening as he leaned forward, arms resting on the desk.

"Gavin!" Spencer's voice was warm, the affection clear. "Good to see you, buddy. Thanks for stopping by." His blue eyes sparkled with his usual charm, and Gavin couldn't help but feel at ease.

"Of course," Gavin replied with a grin. "Amanda said you wanted to talk?"

Spencer nodded, straightening up in his chair. "Yeah, I wanted to check in with you about a few things—mainly how the sales are going. We've had a great quarter so far, and I know you've been handling some of our bigger properties." He paused, folding his hands together. "How are things looking on your end?"

Gavin leaned back in his chair, a confident smile creeping onto his face. "It's been a strong month. The Collins residence had another showing yesterday, and there's real traction there. The clients seemed genuinely interested. I'm expecting to hear back from them by the end of the week." He shifted slightly, excited to share more. "And the Hanover lofts downtown? Those are practically flying off the market. We closed two deals last week, and I've got a few serious offers on the table for the remaining units."

Spencer raised his eyebrows, clearly impressed. "That's fantastic, Gavin. I knew you'd deliver. You've got the magic touch with these high-end listings."

Gavin's grin widened. "It's going well, but what I'm most excited about right now is the lake house. You know, the Riverside Orchid Estate?" He paused for effect, knowing how much this property meant. "We had a showing there earlier this week, and I've never seen clients more captivated by a place. The house practically sells itself."

Spencer's eyes lit up at the mention of the lake house. "Riverside Orchid… now that's a gem. Remind me again, how's it set up?"

Gavin leaned forward, his enthusiasm palpable. "It's a stunning six-bedroom estate right on the water. Open floor plan with floor-to-ceiling windows that look out onto the lake. The main living area has these vaulted ceilings with exposed wooden beams, giving it this warm, rustic, yet modern feel. And the kitchen?" Gavin chuckled. "Top-of-the-line everything—custom cabinetry, calacatta quartz countertops, professional-grade appliances. The master suite has a balcony that overlooks the water, perfect for morning coffee with a view. And did I mention that the deck wraps all the way around the house, leading down to a private dock? The sunset views there are unreal. It's the kind of place that makes you feel like you're on vacation every day."

Spencer nodded, visibly impressed. "That sounds like a dream. And you said the clients were hooked?"

"Completely," Gavin confirmed, his confidence unwavering. "They were already talking about potential décor and layout changes. I wouldn't be surprised if we get an offer within the week."

Spencer sat back, a satisfied smile spreading across his face. "You've really outdone yourself, Gavin. That property is a tough sell given its price point, but if anyone can close it, it's you."

Gavin shrugged modestly. "I'm doing my best. I think it's just a matter of time before we seal the deal."

Spencer leaned forward, his tone softening. "I've got to say, you've been a real asset to the firm. Your instincts are impeccable, and your rapport with clients is something special. You make this job look easy." He paused, his expression turning more personal. "And as a friend? I'm proud of you. I don't think I say it enough, but you're damn good at what you do."

Gavin smiled, feeling a warmth spread through him at Spencer's words. "Thanks, Spence. That means a lot, coming from you."

Spencer stood, walking around the desk to clap Gavin on the shoulder. "I mean it, man. Keep up the good work. The Riverside Orchid deal is going to be huge for both of us. I have no doubt you'll get it done."

Gavin stood as well, nodding. "I'll keep you updated as things progress. Hopefully, we'll be popping some champagne soon."

Spencer chuckled. "I'll hold you to that. Now go on, I'm sure you've got deals to close and clients to charm."

Gavin waved as he made his way out of Spencer's office, feeling a surge of pride. As he returned to his own office, he felt buoyed by their conversation. Spencer had always been a good friend and boss, and the praise he'd just received was exactly the boost Gavin needed to tackle the rest of his day. But as he walked down the hall toward his office, a familiar dread began to settle in his chest—a heaviness that had nothing to do with real estate and everything to do with the secret life he was leading.

He reached his office door and slipped inside, shutting it softly behind him. His office was spacious and refined, with large glass windows that looked out onto the rest of the floor. His desk was a dark walnut masterpiece, always cleaned and organized, just the way he liked it. A few personal touches dotted the room—a framed photo of Eric and Ashton on his desk, a set of bookshelves holding industry awards and certificates, and a minimalist painting that added a pop of color to the otherwise neutral décor.

He glanced out through the glass and saw that his colleagues were busy, heads down, completely absorbed in their own work. *Good.* That meant no one would be eavesdropping on what he was about to do.

Gavin sat at his desk and pulled out his phone. His heart raced as he stared at the screen, Colton's number hovering in front of him. He shouldn't call, not now, not ever. But the temptation was too strong. He needed to hear Colton's voice.

With a quick glance at the door to see no one was in sight for that extra bit of reassurance, Gavin tapped the screen and brought the phone to his ear. It rang twice before Colton picked up.

"It's me," Gavin said, his voice low, almost a whisper.

Colton's reply came immediately, smooth and teasing. "You can't stay away from me, can you?"

Gavin's heart thudded in his chest at the sound of Colton's voice. His tone was always so casual, as if this was nothing more than a game. But to Gavin, it was everything.

Complicated. Messy.

His life was now tangled up in ways he never thought it would be.

"I shouldn't have called," Gavin said, his voice tight. "Things at home are complicated, Colton."

Colton laughed softly on the other end of the line, the sound both comforting and infuriating. "Complicated? You mean *boring*."

Gavin's jaw tightened. "That's not it. Eric—he—"

"Eric doesn't have to know, does he?" Colton interrupted, his voice dripping with confidence. "You keep things so neat and tidy at work, Gavin. Why not let this be the one messy thing in your life? It's not like it'll last forever. You know that."

Gavin swallowed hard, his throat suddenly dry. "I can't just keep doing this. It's going to end badly for the both of us."

"Or you could ride it out," Colton replied, his voice low and seductive. "Enjoy it while it lasts. You *are* enjoying it, aren't you?"

Before Gavin could respond, there was a light knock at his door. His heart jumped into his throat as he quickly lowered his voice. "I have to go," he muttered.

"No, wait—" Colton started, but Gavin cut him off.

"Amanda's here. I'll call you back." He hung up just as the door opened, and Amanda stepped in, holding a beautifully wrapped package in her hands.

"Sorry to interrupt, Gavin, but someone delivered this for you." She smiled, stepping into the room and placing the gift on his desk. It was a square, elegant blue suede jewelry box tied neatly with a matching blue bow. A small card was tucked under the ribbon.

Gavin glanced at the box, confused but intrigued. "Thanks, Amanda," he said, offering her a quick smile as she turned to leave.

As soon as she closed the door behind her, Gavin's attention returned to the gift. He reached out and slid the card from under the ribbon, assuming it was from Colton.

"Sure know how to treat me, huh?" he mumbled to himself, half expecting some flirtatious note from his fling. He peeled the ribbon back and slowly opened the box.

Inside lay a stunning men's bracelet. The design was sleek and modern, with a thick silver band with black accents inlaid around the edges, giving it a masculine yet sophisticated look. The craftsmanship was impeccable—heavy, polished metal and a subtle shimmer that caught the light as he lifted it from its box. It felt cool in his hands, the weight of it suggesting it was expensive, probably custom-made.

But as Gavin reached for the card, a knot formed in his stomach. He flipped it open, and his heart sank.

To my incredible husband.
Thought you'd like this.

Love, Eric.

The words blurred before Gavin's eyes as guilt hit him like a wave, crashing through the thin veil of pleasure and desire he'd been holding onto. This wasn't from Colton at all—it was from Eric, his husband, the man who, even with their busy lives, still thought of him. Still loved him enough to buy him something this special.

Gavin placed the bracelet back in its box, his hands trembling slightly as the weight of his actions settled over him. He was risking everything—his marriage, his family, his life with Eric and Ashton—for what? A fling that would burn out as quickly as it started, just as Colton had said.

He stared at the bracelet, feeling both wonderful and wretched all at once. Eric had no idea. He was at the hospital, saving lives, thinking about Gavin, planning surprises for him—and here Gavin was, leading a double life, one filled with secrets and lies.

The moral dilemma consumed at him. How could he ever wear this bracelet, this token of Eric's love, knowing what he'd been doing behind his husband's back? Yet, at the same time, how could he continue this affair and still look Eric in the eye?

Gavin leaned back in his chair, rubbing a hand over his face. The thrill he once felt from Colton was beginning to sour, turning into something darker that no longer excited him but made him feel hollow inside.

He closed the jewelry box with a soft click and placed it gently in his desk drawer, his heart heavy. He had to make a decision, and he had to make it soon. But for now, all he could do was sit there, staring out at the bustling office floor, feeling more trapped than ever.

Chapter 4

Gavin pulled his shiny black car into the long driveway of the Riverside Orchid Estate, the gravel crunching beneath the tires as the stunning lake house came into full view. The property was as breathtaking as ever, the expansive front lawn meticulously manicured and lined with tall, mature trees that provided both shade and privacy. The house itself was a masterpiece of modern architecture combined with rustic charm—a seamless blend of wood, stone, and glass that perfectly harmonized with the surrounding nature. The lake, shimmering under the late afternoon sun, stretched out behind the house, its gentle waves lapping quietly at the private dock.

As Gavin stepped out of the car, the crisp, cool air of the lakefront hit him, and he took a deep breath, allowing himself to appreciate the property. It was hard not to be impressed by the Riverside Orchid Estate. The expansive six-bedroom home boasted floor-to-ceiling windows, giving every room a view of the serene water. The open floor plan allowed for plenty of natural light to flood in, highlighting the vaulted ceilings with exposed wooden beams and the vast, inviting spaces designed for comfort and luxury.

His client, Leo, exited the car next. A tall, fit man in his late thirties, Leo had an air of quiet confidence. Dressed casually in a light sweater and tailored pants, Leo walked toward Gavin, his eyes scanning the property with careful consideration.

"Beautiful," Leo said, his voice even, but with a hint of admiration. "The pictures didn't quite do it justice."

Gavin smiled, always pleased when a client was impressed by the first glimpse. "I knew you'd like it in person. There's something about being here that just clicks once you see how it's set up. The view, the layout, the lake—it all comes together."

He gestured toward the wide front porch, where the stone pillars and wooden beams framed the entrance to the house. "Shall we?"

Leo nodded, following Gavin up the stone steps and through the grand front door. The entryway opened into a sprawling living space that immediately showcased the home's best feature: the panoramic view of the lake, visible through the expansive windows that lined the back of the house.

Gavin led Leo further into the house, his voice calm, but filled with the practiced confidence of a seasoned real estate agent. "As you can see, this space was designed to let in as much natural light as possible. These windows are custom-made, with UV protection to keep the rooms cool while still letting in the sunlight. You've got your vaulted ceilings here, which really give the space that open, airy feel."

Leo nodded, his eyes roaming the high ceilings and exposed beams, which added a touch of rustic charm. "It's a great balance of modern and traditional," he commented, stepping closer to the windows to take in the full view of the lake. "And the privacy here is exceptional."

Gavin smiled, sensing Leo's growing interest. "Exactly. You've got over two acres of land here, all of it secluded. And, of course, you've got your private dock out back, perfect for boating or just relaxing by the water. The sunsets here are something special—they reflect right off the lake and light up the whole house."

They moved into the kitchen, a chef's dream space with custom cabinetry, state-of-the-art stainless steel appliances, and marble countertops that gleamed in the sunlight. The island in the center of the kitchen was wide and inviting, perfect for hosting large gatherings.

"This kitchen," Gavin said, gesturing with his hand, "is

fully equipped for entertaining. Everything you see here is top-of-the-line. Double ovens, a six-burner range, wine fridge. Plenty of space for prepping meals, and the open layout means you can cook and entertain without feeling closed off from your guests."

Leo ran his hand along the smooth marble countertop, a thoughtful expression on his face. "My husband is the cook between us," he said with a smile. "He'll be interested in seeing this."

Gavin chuckled. "I have a feeling he'll love it. And if you entertain, the layout of this house is perfect for that. The living area flows right into the kitchen and then out onto the deck."

He led Leo through the large sliding doors onto the deck, which wrapped around the house and offered a spectacular view of the lake. "This deck is all weather-resistant, so you'll never have to worry about maintaining it. And it leads right down to the dock. Imagine summer evenings out here with a glass of wine, watching the sunset over the water."

Leo leaned against the railing, nodding thoughtfully. "It's stunning. But the price tag…" He let his sentence trail off, clearly weighing the decision in his mind.

Gavin, sensing the hesitation, kept his tone easy. "The Riverside Orchid Estate is listed at just under three and a half million. It's definitely on the higher end, but given the location, the privacy, and the amenities, I'd say it's a competitive price. The market for lakefront properties like this one has been strong, especially with people looking for homes outside the city. It's an investment, but I have no doubt it will hold its value—and more."

Leo turned to face him, his expression serious. "It's not just the cost, though. My husband… well, he's not as easily swayed by places like this. It'll take some heavy convincing to get him on board."

Gavin nodded, understanding the challenge. "Of course.

These decisions are never just about one person. But this place sells itself once you see the potential. Maybe bring him by for a second showing? Let him get a feel for it in person."

Leo considered this, glancing around once more. "I think you're right. I can be persuasive when I need to be. It's just going to take a little time."

Gavin smiled, appreciating Leo's determination. "I'm confident you'll convince him. And I'm always here if you need me to walk you both through the finer points. I'll make sure he sees the value of this place."

Leo chuckled. "I may just take you up on that." He checked his watch, sighing softly. "I've got to run to another meeting, but I'll definitely be in touch. This is... exactly what I've been looking for."

Gavin walked Leo back through the house and out to the front door, their conversation filled with details about the property and a few personal touches that made the exchange feel more like two friends chatting than a business transaction.

As they reached the driveway, Leo turned to Gavin, offering a firm handshake. "Thanks for showing me the place. I've got a lot to think about, but I'll talk to my husband, and we'll see where we land."

Gavin nodded. "Take your time. I'm here whenever you need me."

Leo gave a final wave as he got into his car, driving off down the gravel driveway. Gavin stood there, watching him go, the weight of the day settling in.

He was ready to head out when he saw an all-to-familiar gray convertible pulling up in the driveway.

Gavin's heart raced as he saw Colton step out of the car. Why was Colton here? How did he know Gavin's schedule? But Gavin would be lying if he said his insides weren't tingling. Colton was like a drug, and Gavin was addicted.

"Hey there, handsome," Colton said with a grin as he approached Gavin.

"Colton, what are you doing here?" Gavin asked, trying to keep his voice steady.

"I'm your next client," Colton replied, winking at Gavin. "I couldn't resist the chance to see you again."

Gavin's pulse quickened as Colton stepped closer, their bodies just inches apart. He could feel the heat radiating off of Colton, and he knew what was coming next.

"We shouldn't," Gavin whispered, even as he leaned in for a kiss.

Colton's lips were soft and warm, and Gavin felt himself melting into the kiss. He knew he shouldn't be doing this but couldn't help himself.

Before he knew it, their clothes were strewn across the living room floor. Colton's hands were all over Gavin's body, touching and caressing him in all the right places.

Gavin sank to his knees, taking Colton's hard cock into his mouth. He sucked and licked, feeling Colton's body tremble with pleasure.

"Fuck, Gavin," Colton moaned, threading his fingers through Gavin's hair. "You're so damn good at that."

Gavin looked up at Colton, their eyes locking as Gavin continued to suck and stroke. He could feel Colton's cock twitching in his mouth, and he knew Colton was close.

Colton pulled Gavin to his feet, not wanting to cum too early before feeling Gavin's warm, tight hole. Colton soon wrapped Gavin into a tight embrace as they passionately kissed and collapsed onto the staged couch in a tangle of limbs. Gavin then flipped his body around so he was on top of Colton, facing away from him. Colton's massive girth was just inches away from his mouth, while Gavin's cock was just a stretch away from Colton's face. They 69ed, each sucking and licking the other's cocks as if their lives depended on it.

Colton took it a step further and began massaging Gavin's smooth hole with his fingertips, ever so slowly, to tease him, before pressing a single finger into him.

Gavin let out a deep yelp, but soon relaxed into it. Colton pulled his finger out and reached for the bottle of lube he brought beside him. He lathered his fingers up and then went to town on Colton's ass with them.

Gavin could feel not only Colton's hot breath on his cock, but also his fingers pulsating in and out of him. He moaned with pleasure, now having almost every single nerve in his body heightened.

"I need you inside me," Gavin gasped, pulling away from Colton's cock.

Colton didn't need to be asked twice. He sat up and held Gavin's body in his arms. He positioned Gavin on top of him, and Gavin slid right down onto Colton's cock without a moment's notice, moaning with pleasure as he felt Colton fill him up.

Gavin rode Colton, their bodies moving in perfect harmony. Colton's hands were on Gavin's hips, guiding him up and down.

"Yes, baby," Gavin growled, his head thrown back in ecstasy. "Yes, fuck me harder."

Colton obliged, now lifting Gavin as he stood up. He began to fuck Gavin in the air, watching Gavin's dick flop and spin like a helicopter propeller while fucking him. Gavin's cock slapped against his stomach with each thrust, and he could feel himself getting closer and closer to the edge.

"I'm gonna cum," Gavin gasped, his body trembling with pleasure.

Colton didn't let up, fucking Gavin harder and faster. Gavin's cock erupted, cum shooting all over his chest.

Colton followed suit, cumming deep inside Gavin.

They stood there, panting and sweaty, their bodies entwined. Gavin knew he should feel guilty, but he didn't. All he felt was pleasure and satisfaction. It was as if he could feel Colton's man milk seep all the way up into his stomach; he shot so hard.

They collapsed onto the couch, their bodies spent and sated. They lay there for a few minutes, catching their breath and basking in the afterglow of their intense lovemaking.

Once they caught their breath, reality struck them. It was time to go once again. They had overstayed their welcome in the Riverside Orchid house.

"I'll see you soon," Colton whispered, kissing Gavin gently on the lips.

Gavin watched as Colton got dressed and left, his body still tingling with pleasure. He knew he shouldn't keep seeing Colton, but couldn't resist the pull.

Colton was his bad habit that he just couldn't seem to break.

Gavin sat behind his desk, staring absently at his laptop screen as sunlight poured in through the floor-to-ceiling windows of his office. His thoughts weren't on the emails waiting for his response or the upcoming property showcases. They were lingering on the night before. His encounter with Colton at the Riverside Orchid Estate played over in his mind like a film reel on repeat, leaving him both exhilarated and heavy with guilt. The heat of the moment had long passed, but the consequences were settling in.

A light knock on the door pulled him from his thoughts. Amanda, the office's ever-efficient assistant, entered without waiting for a response, balancing a stack of documents in one hand and a bright scarlet bag in the other.

"Good morning, Gavin. I've got those contracts you wanted for the Rosewood deal, and, oh, this was left for you at the front desk," she said, placing the documents on his desk and holding out the small bag.

Gavin frowned, not expecting anything. "From who?"

Amanda shrugged. "He didn't want to leave his name.

Just said it was for you."

"Thanks," Gavin muttered, his heart inexplicably speeding up as he took the bag.

Amanda lingered, her eyes shifting to the bag curiously. "Anything else you need?"

"No, that's all. I'll let you know if something comes up. Thank you." Gavin replied, eager to be alone.

Amanda gave him a brief nod and left, her heels clicking against the polished floor as she exited the office. The second she was gone, Gavin pulled the gift bag closer, his hands trembling slightly. He set it on his desk and pulled at the neatly tied bow. The paper crinkled as he reached inside and pulled out the contents. His breath caught in his throat.

A pair of pristine white Calvin Klein underwear tumbled out, folded perfectly, the iconic logo emblazoned on the waistband. A small card was nestled at the bottom of the bag. He hesitated before picking it up, feeling a knot form in his stomach. The note was handwritten, the familiar script instantly recognizable.

Figured I owed you a pair from the night at the park. Can't promise I won't rip this pair too to get to that sexy ass of yours. 😉

Gavin's face burned crimson, his mind immediately racing back to that night—his and Colton's encounter in the secluded park, where the heat of passion had blurred the lines of morality. He had been careless then. Anyone could have run into them there. Now, it felt like his entire world was balancing on the edge of a knife.

He swallowed hard, a mixture of shame and arousal flooding through him as he stared at the note.

What was Colton playing at?

The thought of his boldness sent a shiver down Gavin's

spine. He felt turned on, an undeniable rush spreading through his body, but at the same time, guilt plagued him.

The door to his office creaked open, and Gavin jumped, shoving the underwear and note into the bag hastily. His heart pounded as Spencer walked in, his dark eyes narrowing with a smirk that told Gavin he'd seen more than enough.

"What are you hiding over there, Gav?" Spencer asked, raising an eyebrow. He leaned casually against the doorframe with his arms crossed.

Gavin tried to compose himself, smoothing his hands over his suit. "Nothing. Just some… uh, unexpected mail," he stammered, but he could feel the heat rising in his face again.

Spencer chuckled, walking further into the office. "Right. Sure. I saw that smirk when you were reading the note. Couldn't have been *that innocent*."

Gavin groaned inwardly. "It's nothing, really."

"Look, I saw the guy who dropped it off at the front desk," Spencer said, his voice casual but probing. "Handsome guy, not gonna lie. But it definitely didn't look like how you've described your husband."

The words hung in the air like a loaded gun. Gavin's heart skipped a beat. He glanced at Spencer, unsure how to respond. Spencer knew. But how much did he really know?

Spencer sat down across from him, looking more serious now. "You don't have to tell me anything if you don't want to, but… I've been where you are. I get it."

Gavin's brow furrowed. "What do you mean?"

Spencer exhaled, leaning back in the chair. "Getting attention from someone outside your marriage. It feels… *electric*, doesn't it? Hearing things you haven't heard from your spouse in years. Feeling wanted in a way that makes you feel alive again. But, Gavin, things can spiral fast. And they rarely end well."

Gavin stared at him, the weight of Spencer's words sinking in. He looked away, feeling both ashamed and exposed.

Spencer continued, his tone softer now. "A seductor and someone else who is vulnerable... It's a deadly combination, trust me. I've been in your shoes before. I know how easy it is to get swept up in it. It's like a drug, man."

Gavin swallowed the lump forming in his throat. "So, how did you... overcome it? The other guy. His charm, all the attention?"

Spencer's expression darkened. "I started seeing a shrink. Dr. Henry Jacobs. He's good—really helped me get my head straight. But, to be honest, I didn't overcome it before things went too far. It nearly cost me my marriage, my family, everything."

Gavin's stomach twisted. Spencer, always the level-headed, charming friend, had gone through this? He felt a pang of fear, realizing he was standing on the same precipice.

"Well, you seem to be doing well now..." Gavin ventured, unsure what else to say.

"Yeah," Spencer said with a grim smile. "But I had to lose everything first. Trust me, Gavin, whatever you're getting from this guy, it's not worth it. You've got too much to lose."

Gavin's heart sank. He thought of Eric, his son Ashton, and the family he was slowly dismantling with each secret encounter. But there was a part of him that still craved what Colton had given him—something raw, something dangerous. Something Eric hadn't given him in years.

Spencer stood up, placing a hand on Gavin's shoulder. "Think about it before it's too late. At least have a quick conversation with Dr. Jacobs. See how it is. Believe me, it will do you wonders."

As Spencer left the office, Gavin stared at the gift bag and the Calvin Klein underwear hidden inside. He clenched his jaw, the weight of his choices pressing down on him. How much longer could he juggle this secret life before everything came crashing down?

Chapter 5

The late afternoon sun cast a golden hue over the baseball field in the suburbs, the day's warmth slowly giving way to the cool breeze of early evening. The field was alive with energy—parents crowded the bleachers, kids in bright uniforms scurried about, and the smell of fresh grass and dirt mixed with the scent of hot dogs and popcorn from the nearby concession stand lingered. The clamor of chatter and excitement filled the air, blending with the occasional crack of a bat hitting a ball and the enthusiastic shouts of coaches urging their players forward.

Gavin sat on the wooden bleachers, perched near the edge, his phone in hand as he prepared to take pictures. The old, slightly worn-down seats creaked beneath the weight of cheering parents, but Gavin hardly noticed. His eyes were locked on the field, specifically on Ashton, who stood at home plate, his tiny hands gripping the bat tightly, his knuckles white with concentration. Ashton was dressed in his team's uniform—a white jersey with blue lettering and a matching blue cap that sat slightly askew on his head.

Gavin smiled as he watched his son nervously shift his feet in the dirt, digging his cleats just like Eric had shown him. Gavin's husband stood on third base as an assistant coach, his figure tall and steady as he waited for the next play to give his players directional instructions on whether or not to run or stay on base. The sight of Eric there, his long-time steady presence, made Gavin feel a swell of pride. His husband looked so confident in his role, coaching and guiding the young players with that same dedication he brought to everything else. These were the kinds of moments that Gavin cherished, where their family felt like the center of the world, connected by shared experiences.

The umpire's voice cut through the noise, calling the next pitch. Ashton was up to bat. Gavin leaned forward, gripping his phone tighter as he prepared for the camera shot, hoping it would capture a successful hit.

"Come on, Ash!" Gavin shouted, his voice filled with encouragement. "You've got this, buddy!"

The pitch came fast, and Ashton swung with all his might—but the bat cut through the air, missing the ball entirely. The sharp sound of the umpire calling out, "Strike one!" echoed through the field.

Ashton froze, visibly frustrated, and Gavin could see the nervousness in his son's small frame. The crowd murmured, a mix of support and tension, but Gavin stayed focused. He knew Ashton had more in him.

"That's alright, Ash!" Gavin yelled from the bleachers, clapping his hands. "Shake it off and focus, kiddo! You've got this!"

From his spot on third base, Eric pointed toward Ashton and shouted his own encouragement. "Just watch the ball, Ash! Nice and easy!"

Ashton adjusted his stance, his little shoulders rising as he took a deep breath, determination now evident in his posture. The next pitch came in, and this time, Ashton swung with precision. The bat made solid contact, and the ball flew up into the air, sailing just over the infield.

Gavin jumped to his feet, his phone forgotten for a second, as the crowd erupted into cheers. Ashton darted toward first base, his legs pumping furiously as he rounded the bag and made his way to second. Gavin quickly snapped a few pictures, pride surging through him as he watched his son make it safely to second base.

"Yes! That's how you do it!" Gavin cheered, his voice mixing with the roar of the crowd. Parents around him clapped and hollered, some standing and waving as the energy in the stands reached a fever pitch. Gavin's fingers fumbled with his phone, snapping shot after shot of Ashton, who was beaming from his spot on second, his blue helmet barely clinging to his head.

Gavin couldn't help but grin. *This is what it's all about*, he thought. Building memories like these, watching Ashton grow, learn, and succeed, surrounded by those who loved him. It made everything worthwhile—the long days, the challenges at work, even the complications in his personal life. Here, on this field, everything felt simple and pure.

Another batter stepped up to the plate, and the crowd quieted, the tension building once more. Gavin could feel his pulse quicken as the pitcher wound up and threw. The bat cracked, and the ball flew, rolling deep into the outfield. Ashton took off, running hard, his little legs carrying him as fast as they could.

Eric was already pointing and waving his arm with excitement. "Go, Ashton, go!" he shouted, his voice carrying over the noise. "Keep running! All the way home!"

Gavin watched, his heart racing as Ashton rounded third base, his face red with effort but determined to make it. Eric's voice was full of energy, urging him on as the ball was hurriedly thrown toward home plate.

Ashton didn't hesitate. He charged toward home, the crowd roaring with encouragement as he slid into home plate. Dust kicked up around him as his cleats dug into the dirt. The ball zipped toward the catcher, but it was too late.

"Safe!" the umpire shouted, his arms spread wide.

The crowd exploded into cheers, and Gavin's throat tightened with emotion as he watched his son scramble to his feet, his face lit up with pure joy. Ashton waved to the crowd, searching for Gavin in the sea of faces, and when their eyes finally met, they exchanged an endearing smile.

Gavin couldn't stop smiling, his heart full to the brim as he waved back, snapping more pictures of Ashton, his pride evident in every camera click. In that instant, Gavin felt overwhelmed by how much he loved this life and this family. Sure, things were complicated—messy, even—but nothing could compare to the happiness he felt seeing Ashton's smile or the way Eric beamed at their son from across the field. It was everything he had ever wanted and more.

But as Gavin snapped the final shot, a strange sensation crept over him. His skin prickled, and the hairs on the back of his neck stood on end as if someone was watching him. He lowered his phone and glanced around, but the crowd was still buzzing with excitement; everyone was too caught up in the game to pay any attention to him.

He shrugged it off, telling himself it was just his nerves, but little did he know someone *was* watching him—carefully, from a distance.

Parked in a car near the edge of the lot, partially hidden by the line of trees, a camera lens was pointed directly at him. Its shutter clicked quietly as it captured each of Gavin's movements. The figure behind the camera remained hidden in the shadows, snapping shot after shot, unseen by Gavin or anyone else.

As Gavin shifted his attention to the game, still caught up in the thrill of Ashton's success, the camera clicked one last time before the car pulled away, leaving the baseball field behind as silently as it had arrived.

The soft hum of ambient music drifted through the air as Gavin stepped into Dr. Henry Jacobs' office that evening after Ashton's baseball game. The waiting room was warm and inviting, with soft lighting that gave the space an almost serene, spa-like quality. Pale green walls, adorned with abstract minimalist art, framed the room, and a thick beige rug covered the hardwood floor, muffling the sound of Gavin's steps. A few leather chairs were scattered around, and a table in the middle held neatly arranged magazines. The scent of lavender lingered in the air, calming yet making Gavin feel slightly on edge. This wasn't a place he ever imagined he'd be, but his boss, Spencer, had insisted Dr. Jacobs could help.

Gavin was greeted by Dr. Henry Jacobs himself. He was tall and slightly built, with salt-and-pepper hair and dark-framed glasses that made him look both intellectual and approachable. He wore a casual blazer over a button-up shirt, his demeanor relaxed and welcoming as he extended a hand.

"Gavin, it's good to meet you. Thanks for coming on short notice," Dr. Jacobs said with a warm smile, gesturing toward the office door.

"No worries," Gavin replied, shaking the doctor's hand. "I appreciate you making time for me. Spencer spoke highly of you, and well... I needed to talk to someone."

"Any friend of Spencer's," Dr. Jacobs said with a soft chuckle as they stepped into the office. The room was even cozier than the waiting area, with a large window letting in natural light. A soft, plush couch sat across from an armchair, a small table between them with a box of tissues resting on top. Dr. Jacobs gestured for Gavin to sit on the couch.

Gavin settled in, feeling the weight of the cushions beneath him, and took a deep breath. He glanced around the room. There were no imposing degrees on the wall, no cold, clinical air about the place. Instead, the shelves were filled with books, small sculptures, and a few framed photos, all adding a personal touch. It was a comfortable space designed to make someone open up.

"So," Dr. Jacobs began as he sat in the chair opposite Gavin, his voice calm and reassuring. "What brings you in today? Spencer mentioned you were going through something, but didn't give me any details."

Gavin exhaled slowly, his hands resting on his knees. "It's

complicated," he started, unsure of how to even begin. "I'm married. Have been for years. My husband, Eric, and I have a son, Ashton. He's eight. Everything should be perfect, right?"

Dr. Jacobs nodded slightly, his expression open, encouraging Gavin to continue.

"But it's not," Gavin said, his voice lowering. "Because I've been having an affair."

The words hung in the air, and Dr. Jacobs didn't flinch, his gaze steady but nonjudgmental.

"With someone named Colton," Gavin continued, running a hand through his hair. "And I don't trust myself around him. Whenever I think I can walk away, I get pulled right back in. He's... I don't know. It's more than just sex."

Dr. Jacobs leaned forward slightly, his eyes focused on Gavin. "You said you can't seem to pull away from Colton. What is it about him that draws you in?"

Gavin hesitated, his gaze dropping to the floor. "The sex is... *intense*. It's wild, almost animalistic. Everything with him is raw and untamed. It's exciting in ways that... well, that it isn't with Eric." He felt a flush rise to his cheeks, embarrassed by the admission, but he forced himself to continue. "But that's not all of it. If it were just sex, I wouldn't be sitting here right now. I'd walk away with no problems. But I just seem to can't."

Dr. Jacobs studied Gavin before speaking. "If that's all it is, it should be an easy decision to walk away, no?"

Gavin shook his head. "It's not that simple. It can't just be sex. If it was, I wouldn't be in this office right now. I could easily walk away."

"Maybe," Dr. Jacobs mused, crossing one leg over the other, "you love two men and find yourself stuck in a dilemma where you have to choose. Could it be that you're trying to navigate between your love for both of them?"

Gavin immediately shook his head. "Oh no. It's not like that. I could never be in a *real* relationship with Colton. He's not husband material. Colton's... he's a player, full-time. But the crazy thing is, he does love me. I know he does."

Dr. Jacobs' brow furrowed slightly, intrigued. "That could be a powerful allure. A challenge, even. Maybe you're chasing something you know you can't fully have. Are you sure that's not it? That you're not trying to change Colton's ways, trying to make him someone who's just for you?"

Gavin scoffed, though his voice was tinged with uncertainty. "No! Absolutely not. I'm not trying to change him. I know who he is. And I love my family. Eric and Ashton... they mean everything to me. I'd never risk losing them."

Dr. Jacobs leaned back slightly, his expression thoughtful. "And yet you're risking losing them with this affair. That's why you're here, isn't it?"

Gavin's shoulders slumped, the weight of his guilt finally crashing down on him. "That's what scares me the most. I know I'm risking everything. That's why I'm here, because I know this can't keep going. But I can't stop." His voice trembled as he admitted the truth. "Spencer said you helped him through some tough times, and I thought... maybe you could help me."

Dr. Jacobs was silent, letting Gavin's words settle in the air. Finally, he spoke, his voice measured and calm. "What you're experiencing isn't unusual, Gavin. It's not uncommon to feel pulled in two different directions, especially when one offers something your current relationship doesn't. But you need to ask yourself what you really want, deep down."

Gavin's eyes shifted, staring blankly at a spot on the floor. "I want my family. I want Eric. I love him. But with Colton... it's like I lose control. I don't think straight. I make stupid decisions, and I hate myself for it afterward. But when I'm with him... it feels so good, so... *free*."

Dr. Jacobs nodded. "That sense of freedom, that rush—it can be intoxicating. But it's fleeting. If you want to work through this, it's going to take some hard decisions. You need to figure out whether this affair is something you're willing to end to preserve what you've built with Eric and Ashton. Or… if you're chasing something in Colton that you'll never truly find anywhere else."

Gavin swallowed hard, feeling the weight of the conversation pressing down on him. He looked up, meeting Dr. Jacobs' eyes. "I honestly don't know if I'm strong enough to walk away."

Dr. Jacobs offered a small, empathetic smile. "You're stronger than you think, Gavin. The fact that you're here, that you recognize the danger in what you're doing, is the first step. Now it's about figuring out how to take the next one."

Gavin nodded slowly, unsure of where this would all lead, but knowing that something had to change. The stakes were too high. And as much as the pull toward Colton was tempting, Gavin realized, deep down, that the most important thing was right in front of him—his family.

"Thank you, Dr. Jacobs," Gavin said softly, feeling a slight sense of relief. "I needed this."

Dr. Jacobs gave a reassuring nod. "We'll work through it. One step at a time."

Chapter 6

The art gallery was buzzing with life, lively conversation filling the air as patrons moved between exhibits, pausing to admire the artwork on display. The space was modern and vast, with high ceilings and stark white walls that provided the perfect backdrop for the vibrant paintings and sculptures scattered throughout. Spotlights were carefully angled to highlight each piece, casting soft shadows that added depth to the collection. The air was tinged with the scent of fresh paint, and the earthy undertone of wood blended with the more refined aroma of expensive perfume and cologne from the guests.

Gavin stood near the entrance, surveying the room. He tugged at the collar of his tailored suit, adjusting it slightly, before making his way toward the bar. The bar itself was a polished affair—smooth black granite with backlit shelving that showcased an array of top-shelf liquor in glowing hues of amber and crystal. Tall martini glasses were lined up neatly on the counter, waiting to be filled, while the bartender, dressed impeccably in black, mixed drinks with a practiced flair.

"I'll take an extra dirty vodka martini," Gavin said as he reached the bar, his voice low and smooth.

"How extra is *extra*?" the bartender asked. "Are we talking about *Playboy TV* or *Cinemax* dirty?"

Gavin playfully shook his head. "More like an *HBO After Dark* martini. Slightly dirty, but not so vulgar."

The bartender nodded. "Totally got it!" he replied, before swiftly preparing the drink. Gavin watched as the olive brine swirled into the glass, the drink turning cloudy as the vodka and vermouth mixed. The bartender slid the martini over with a smile, placing a thin metal pick speared through three olives as a final touch.

Gavin took a sip, the sharp, salty bite of the martini hitting his tongue just right. He let the cool liquid roll over his taste buds, then started to stroll through the gallery, the soft thrum of the event fading slightly into the background as his attention shifted.

He'd come to see Colton's work. Of course, Colton was the reason he was here at all. His eyes wandered the gallery until they landed on a set of large canvases near the far wall, where a crowd had gathered. Gavin navigated his way through the group, his heart already beginning to race.

Colton's artwork was bold—raw, chaotic, and utterly mesmerizing. The first piece Gavin stood before was a massive canvas splattered with thick, vibrant strokes of crimson, cobalt, and gold. The colors bled into one another, the jagged lines and aggressive brushwork creating a sense of movement that was almost violent. It was like watching a storm captured mid-fury, energy and tension wrapped into a single frame.

The next painting was more subdued, yet just as intense—a figure, barely discernible, hidden within layers of thick, textured paint. There was something haunting about the way the shadows played against the lighter streaks, suggesting a form struggling to emerge. It was as if Colton had painted someone trying to break free, yet held back by invisible chains. Gavin could feel the turmoil behind each stroke, the deep, almost primal emotions that bled through the canvas.

"Admiring my work?"

Gavin's heart skipped a beat at the familiar voice behind him. He turned to find Colton standing there, his lips curled into a knowing smile. Colton, dressed in a perfectly fitted black shirt that hugged his frame just right, exuded a mix of confidence and artistic panache. His dark hair was slightly tousled, giving him a roguish, effortlessly cool look.

"Hard not to," Gavin replied, trying to maintain a calm exterior. "Your work is... *intense*. I can see why it's drawing so much attention."

Colton stepped closer, his gaze locked on Gavin. "You should know by now—intensity is kind of my thing."

Gavin chuckled, taking another sip of his martini as he glanced at the nearest painting. "You've outdone yourself with this one," he said, gesturing to the stormy canvas. "It's chaotic, but there's something underneath. Like there's more to it than meets the eye."

Colton raised an eyebrow, clearly impressed. "You've been paying attention. Most people just see the mess."

"I don't think I've ever been able to see you as just a mess," Gavin said quietly, his voice barely above a whisper.

Colton's eyes darkened slightly, his lips curving into a sly grin. "Careful. You're starting to sound like you missed me."

Before Gavin could reply, Colton took his arm and pulled him away from the main gallery, leading him down a quiet hallway off to the side, where the noise of the crowd faded into the background. The hallway was lined with a few smaller, more intimate pieces—mostly sketches and charcoal drawings—but Colton wasn't interested in them. He turned to Gavin, his expression playful but laced with something deeper.

"I didn't expect to see you here tonight," Colton said, leaning casually against the wall, his eyes fixed on Gavin with that familiar magnetic intensity. "I figured you'd be stuck with the husband and kid."

Gavin smirked, swirling his martini lazily. "I told them I had an emergency appointment with a client—a showing I couldn't miss. Eric and Ashton went to our beach house for the weekend. I told them I'd join them tomorrow."

Colton's grin widened, and he let out a low, amused laugh. "Wow. You are wicked."

Gavin shrugged, his voice calm but with an undercurrent of excitement. "I had to see your show. And I knew I wouldn't be able to get away if I didn't come up with a plausible excuse."

Colton stepped closer, his voice dropping to a whisper. "And here I thought you'd never lie to the family."

Gavin's heart raced as Colton moved into his personal space. He felt the warmth radiating off Colton's body, the intoxicating closeness pulling him in. "Sometimes," Gavin said softly, "you have to bend the truth."

Colton's eyes fluttered with amusement. "And what would Eric say if he knew where you were right now?"

Gavin met Colton's gaze, a flicker of guilt dancing across his features, but he pushed it down. "He won't. I'll be at the beach tomorrow, pretending like nothing eventful happened."

Colton laughed, shaking his head in disbelief. "You're something else, Gavin. I didn't think you had it in you."

"It's not like I'm proud of it," Gavin said, a bit more defensively than he intended. "But I'm here now, aren't I?"

Colton's hand brushed lightly against Gavin's arm, his touch electric. "Oh, you're definitely here," he enticingly uttered. "And that's all that matters."

Gavin swallowed hard, torn between the thrill of this instance and the ever-present guilt that gnawed at him. His mind wandered back to the painting on the wall—trapped mayhem, a storm that couldn't quite break free. It felt eerily close to what he was experiencing now.

Colton leaned in, his lips hovering just inches from Gavin's ear. "You're playing a dangerous game, Gavin. And I think you like it."

Gavin closed his eyes for a brief second, his breath catching in his throat. "Maybe I do," he admitted quietly. "But this can't last forever."

Colton's grin softened, but there was still mischief in his eyes. "We'll see about that."

Before Gavin could respond, a noise from down the hall

interrupted their moment of intimacy—a small group of patrons wandering closer to the hallway where they stood.

Gavin stepped back, his gaze lingering on Colton before he gave a casual nod toward the crowd. "You'd better get back out there. Don't want to raise any suspicions, right?"

Colton nodded, his mind still spinning from the encounter as he took a slow breath. "Actually…" As Colton began to express his thoughts, he checked the crowd one last time to make sure no one was watching them. Then, he suddenly grabbed Gavin's hand and dragged him towards the emergency exit.

"Wh-Where are we going?" Gavin asked, shocked at Colton's behavior in just leaving his own art show.

"Back to my place. I'm kidnapping you for the night, whether you like it or not," Colton replied.

"You're seriously leaving your art show for me?" Gavin asked.

"Sometimes, you know when to make the right sacrifices," Colton responded.

All Gavin could do was roll his eyes and smile, secretly wanting to be kidnapped by this fucking sexy artistic man who now prioritized him over everything else in his life.

The city was alive as Gavin and Colton stepped out of the gallery, the cool evening air a sharp contrast to the warmth of the crowded room they had just left. The streets were still whirring with energy—taxi cabs weaving through traffic, people laughing and talking as they spilled out of bars and restaurants, and the buzz of neon signs flickering to life above storefronts. Gavin's thoughts were a whirl of emotion, his heart racing as he walked beside Colton, their shoulders brushing slightly with each step.

They didn't talk much as they made their way to Colton's studio apartment, which was only a few blocks from the gallery. The silence between them was charged, full of unspoken tension, the kind that Gavin had grown used to when he was around Colton. It was the type of silence that said more than words ever could. It wasn't long before they arrived at Colton's building—a modest, old brick structure tucked away on a quiet side street. The exterior was unassuming, the sort of place you might walk by without noticing.

Inside, the atmosphere shifted immediately. Colton's apartment reflected him in every sense—artistic, chaotic, but somehow intimate and raw. The space was open and loft-like, with exposed brick walls and oversized industrial windows that let in the soft glow of the city lights outside. There was a single partition that separated the bedroom from the rest of the place. Otherwise, it was just an open floor plan that made the space feel both expansive and personal. The hardwood floors were scuffed and worn, adding a rugged charm to the place, and the walls were covered with sketches, paintings, and half-finished canvases leaning against each other in a sort of organized frenzy.

An easel stood in one corner, with a half-completed painting still resting on it, brushes scattered on the nearby table, their bristles stiff with dried paint. The smell of oil and turpentine lingered faintly in the air, mixing with the earthy scent of the old wood. A small kitchen was off to the side, simple and functional, with just enough room for a tiny stove, a fridge, and some open shelving that held mismatched dishes and wine glasses.

Colton moved across the room with ease, tossing his keys onto a nearby counter and gesturing toward the small bar cart that sat near the kitchen. "Wine?" he asked, already knowing the answer.

Gavin nodded, his eyes wandering around the space. He had been here before, but each time, it felt like stepping into a

THE TROMPE L'OEIL EFFECT

different world—a world far removed from the clean, orderly life he led at home. This place was raw and unfiltered, and it made him feel both on edge and alive.

Colton reached for a bottle of red wine, its dark label worn. He expertly uncorked it and poured two glasses, handing one to Gavin with a small smile. "To another night of making questionable choices," Colton said, his voice low and playful as he clinked his glass against Gavin's.

Gavin smirked, taking a sip of the wine. It was rich and bold, the perfect complement to the tension between them. "Questionable choices seem to be my specialty these days," he replied, glancing down at his glass and watching the deep red liquid swirl before taking another sip.

Colton's eyes gleamed with amusement as he leaned back against the counter, his gaze never leaving Gavin. "I like that about you," he said, his tone both teasing and sincere. "You play the part of the perfect husband, the successful real estate agent, but underneath, you're just as messy as the rest of us."

Gavin let out a short laugh, shaking his head. "You make it sound like it's something to be proud of."

"Maybe it is," Colton replied with a shrug, taking another sip of his wine. "Maybe it's better to be honest about who we really are instead of pretending to be something we're not."

Gavin didn't respond right away; instead, he let the words hang in the air as he wandered over to the large windows that overlooked the city. The lights outside twinkled like stars, casting a soft glow into the room. He felt the familiar pull—the attraction to this world, to Colton, to the disorder and unpredictability of it all.

Before long, Colton moved closer, his footsteps soft against the hardwood floors. He stood beside Gavin, their arms nearly touching as they both stared out at the city beyond the glass. The silence between them was comfortable now, and Colton finally broke it with a question that lingered in the space like smoke.

"So, what's next for you, Gavin? Headed down to the beach house tomorrow, back to playing the family man?"

Gavin sighed, his breath fogging up the glass before he turned to face Colton. "Yeah. Eric and Ashton are expecting me. They're already down there."

Colton grinned, a wicked gleam in his eyes. "You're so good at this. I'm impressed. Lying with such ease."

Gavin's lips twitched into a smile, but it didn't quite reach his eyes. "I wouldn't exactly call it a talent. More like a necessity at this point."

Colton leaned in closer, his voice dropping to a near whisper. "You know, we could stay here all night if you wanted. Forget the rest of the world exists."

Gavin's pulse quickened, but he forced a casual shrug. "I don't know. You've got your art, and I've got my responsibilities."

Colton tilted his head, studying Gavin with a curious intensity. "Responsibilities are overrated. But I get it. You love them. Your family, I mean."

Gavin nodded, taking another sip of his wine. "They mean everything to me," he admitted softly. "That's why I can't keep doing this."

Colton's expression softened, but his voice still had that playful edge. "But you do keep doing it. You keep coming back."

Gavin looked at him, his eyes conflicted. "Yeah. I do."

The two men stood in silence before Colton gestured toward the bed on the far side of the apartment. It was unmade, the sheets rumpled, and it sat low to the ground—simple and practical, much like everything else in Colton's apartment. A few paint-stained clothes were strewn across a nearby chair, and a canvas leaned against the wall, half-painted and abandoned.

"Come on," Colton said, his voice lighter now. "Let's sit."

They both walked over and sat on the edge of the bed,

their wine glasses still in hand. The mattress dipped slightly under their weight, and Gavin could feel the warmth of Colton's body close to his. The tension between them was palpable, but they simply sipped their wine, letting the night settle around them.

"You ever think about just... not going back?" Colton asked, his tone half-serious, half-teasing.

Gavin looked at him, shaking his head. "That's not an option. I told you, my family—Eric, Ashton—they're my life."

Colton leaned back on his hands, a playful smirk on his lips. "And yet, here you are."

Gavin swallowed, his throat tight. "Yeah. Here I am."

They sat like that for a while longer, the city lights strobing through the windows as the night deepened. The weight of their choices and secrets hung in the air, thick and heavy.

Colton's fingers traced a slow path up Gavin's thigh, inching closer and closer to the growing bulge in his pants. "Do you want me to touch you?"

Gavin's breath hitched, his hips involuntarily thrusting forward. "Yes."

Colton's hand closed around Gavin's cock, and he squeezed gently, his touch sending a jolt of pleasure through Gavin's body. "Do you want me to make you feel good?"

Gavin nodded, his eyes fluttering closed. "Yes."

Colton's lips found Gavin's neck, and he kissed him softly, his tongue tracing a slow path up to Gavin's ear. "Do you want me to make you forget your responsibilities?"

Gavin moaned, his hips bucking upward as Colton's hand began to move in a slow, teasing rhythm. "Yes."

Colton's teeth grazed Gavin's earlobe, and he whispered, "Say it."

Gavin's breath was coming in short, sharp gasps now. "Yes, I want you to make me forget."

Colton's eyes widened with excitement, and he placed his wine glass on the nightstand next to the bed. Gavin did the same, turning their full attention to each other.

Gavin leaned in and captured Colton's lips in a passionate kiss. Their tongues intertwined as they explored each other's mouths with fervent desire. Gavin's hands found their way to Colton's toned ass, and he began to knead the firm flesh.

Colton broke the kiss and gazed deeply into Gavin's eyes. He whispered, "Take off your shirt. I want to see your hot body."

Gavin eagerly complied, revealing his chiseled abs and broad shoulders. Colton couldn't help but let out a low moan as he took in the sight of Gavin's naked torso.

Colton's animalistic desire took over, causing him to take complete control. He pushed Gavin down onto the bed and couldn't help but let out a low growl.

Gavin looked up at Colton and seductively bit his lower lip. He whispered, "Take me right here. I want to feel your cock inside me."

Colton's eyes darkened with lust, and he quickly unbuttoned and unzipped Gavin's pants, revealing his hard, throbbing cock.

Colton wasted no time in wrapping his lips around Gavin's engorged member. He began to suck and stroke Gavin's cock with an expert touch, eliciting moans of pleasure from him. Gavin's hands tangled in Colton's hair as he urged him on, desperate for more.

As Colton continued to pleasure Gavin with his mouth, he reached down and began to play with Gavin's ass. He gently probed Gavin's tight hole with his fingers, preparing him for what was to come.

Gavin let out a series of low, guttural moans as Colton expertly worked his cock and ass. He couldn't help but beg for more. "Please, babe. I need you inside me. Fuck me hard."

Colton could no longer resist the temptation, and he quickly stood up and stripped out of his own pants. His own cock stood at attention, eager for the pleasure that awaited them both.

Colton positioned himself behind Gavin, who was now lying fully naked on the bed. He then caught sight and admired Gavin's supple, toned body before him. Gavin looked back at Colton and spread his legs wide, inviting Colton to take him inside his tight, eager ass.

Colton positioned the head of his cock at Gavin's entrance and began to gently push his way inside. Gavin's eyes widened with pleasure as he felt Colton's thick member gradually fill him up.

Colton began to thrust his hips back and forth with slow, deliberate movements. He wanted to savor every minute of their passionate union. Gavin let out a series of low moans as Colton began to pick up the pace, driving his cock deeper and deeper inside Gavin's willing hole.

The sound of their skin slapping together filled the dimly lit room, accompanied by the sounds of their heavy breathing and the low moans they both let out. Colton could feel his orgasm building within him, and he knew that it wouldn't be long before he exploded deep inside Gavin's waiting ass.

Colton began to thrust harder and faster, his hips moving with a rough, animalistic fervor. Gavin let out a series of deep grunts as Colton mercilessly pounded his ass.

"Oh, fuck, Colton! Yes, just like that! Harder, harder, yes!" Gavin cried out, his voice filled with pleasure and desire.

Colton could feel his orgasm building within him, and he knew that it wouldn't be long before he bred Gavin.

"I'm gonna cum, Gavin!" Colton growled through gritted teeth. "You're gonna make me cum so fucking hard!"

"Do it! Fill me up! I want to feel you explode deep inside me!" Gavin cried out, his voice filled with lust and desire.

Colton could no longer hold back, and he slammed his hips forward with a final, powerful thrust. He let out a low, raspy groan as he felt his cock throb and pulse deep inside

Gavin's eager hole. His orgasm was intense and overwhelming, leaving him breathless and trembling.

Gavin felt Colton's warm, sticky cum fill him up, and he couldn't help but let out a series of gravelly moans as he felt Colton's cock twitch and pulse deep inside him. He knew that he had succeeded in his mission to make Colton cum harder than he'd ever experienced before.

Colton slowly pulled his cock out of Gavin's ass, leaving them both breathless and trembling. Their bodies were slick with sweat, and their hearts pounded in their chests.

Colton collapsed his head onto his pillow next to Gavin, and they both lay there in silence, simply basking in the afterglow of their passionate encounter.

Finally, Gavin broke the silence. He turned to Colton and whispered, "That was incredible."

Colton smiled at Gavin and replied, "I couldn't agree more."

As they lay in the bed, their bodies still recovering in sweat and their hearts still pounding in their chests, they both knew this intense love affair wasn't ending anytime soon.

Chapter 7

The sun was beginning to set as Gavin drove back into town after an unforgettable weekend at the beach house with Eric and Ashton. The house, nestled along the coast, had been their sanctuary—a place where they could escape the pressures of city life and just enjoy one another. The weekend had been perfect: days spent playing in the sand with Ashton, laughing as they built elaborate sandcastles and chased waves, and nights spent cozied up on the deck with Eric and a bottle of expensive red wine, watching the sun sink into the horizon.

Gavin smiled to himself as he recalled those instants. Eric had been more affectionate than usual, and their connection felt as solid as ever. The two of them had stolen quiet, romantic moments—holding hands as they walked along the beach, sharing long kisses in the warm sea breeze, wrapping themselves in blankets under the stars, just talking about life. The love between them felt renewed and stronger. It was everything Gavin wanted—everything he feared losing.

But now, back in the city, the demands of his life as a high-end real estate agent quickly began to pull him back into a different mindset. He had an important showing that afternoon, a new penthouse that had just hit the market, and he needed to be fully focused. The beach, the laughter, and the quiet occasions with Eric were now memories tucked away in the back of his mind as he stepped into the professional role he knew so well.

The building where the penthouse was located stood tall in the heart of the city, its vast glass exterior glinting in the late afternoon light. Gavin entered the lobby, his designer shoes tapping softly against the marble floors as he approached the private elevator. He was meeting a new client—a tech entrepreneur looking to purchase a penthouse with both luxury and privacy. Gavin had a feeling this particular place would check all the boxes.

The elevator doors opened smoothly, and Gavin stepped into the expansive penthouse. He took in the space as he waited for the client, feeling a sense of pride. The penthouse was stunning, exactly what one would expect from a property at this price point. The ceilings were high, and the floor-to-ceiling windows offered breathtaking views of the city skyline, the fading sunlight casting long shadows across the modern, open layout.

The living area gave very bachelor pad vibes with black-and-white furniture—leather sofas, glass coffee tables, and a large, abstract painting that stretched across one wall. The smooth concrete floors were softened by strategically placed rugs that added warmth to the modern space. Off to the side, the kitchen gleamed with cutting-edge appliances, white quartz countertops, and a massive island in the center, perfect for entertaining. It was both elegant and inviting, with high-end finishes and a design that seamlessly blended style with comfort.

The sound of the elevator pinged, and Gavin turned as his client, a sharp-dressed man in his early fifties, stepped into the room.

"Jonathan, welcome," Gavin said, extending his hand.

"Thanks, Gavin," Jonathan replied, shaking his hand firmly. "I've heard great things about this place. I can't wait to see it."

Gavin smiled confidently, leading the man further into the penthouse. "You won't be disappointed. This is one of the most sought-after properties in the city right now. You've got over thirty-five hundred square feet of living space, and as you can see, these windows give you unobstructed views. You'll get natural light all day."

The client glanced around, nodding in approval. "It's

definitely got the wow factor. How's the privacy?"

"Top-notch," Gavin said, gesturing toward the windows. "This floor is private access, so you won't have to deal with neighbors, and the building's security is state-of-the-art. You've got 24/7 concierge services, too. And if you look outside here," Gavin guided him toward the balcony, "this is one of the largest private terraces in the city."

The terrace was expansive, stretching across the entire width of the penthouse, with slender glass railings that didn't obstruct the view. It was perfect for outdoor entertaining, with space for a lounge area, dining set, and even a fire pit.

"This is incredible," Jonathan said, his voice filled with admiration as he took in the view. "I can already picture having friends and clients over for drinks out here."

Gavin smiled, sensing Jonathan's interest. "It's perfect for that. You're also just steps away from some of the best dining and nightlife in the city. But with this view, I imagine you'll want to spend most of your evenings right here."

They spent the next several minutes walking through the rest of the penthouse—large bedrooms with ensuite bathrooms, a fully equipped home office, and a media room that was perfect for movie nights or business presentations. Gavin highlighted the modern features and custom finishes, knowing exactly how to appeal to a buyer like Jonathan Fields.

When they finished the tour, Jonathan turned to Gavin, clearly impressed. "This place is exactly what I've been looking for. I need to talk it over with my wife, but I'm pretty sold."

"Take your time," Gavin said smoothly, knowing the importance of not rushing a decision at this price point. "I'll follow up with you in a couple of days. If you have any questions in the meantime, just let me know."

They shook hands again, and Jonathan Fields left with a satisfied expression on his face. Gavin watched him disappear into the elevator before he stepped outside, ready to head back to his office.

As soon as he stepped out onto the quiet street, though, the familiar prickling sensation returned—the same uncomfortable feeling he'd had over the past several days like someone was watching him. His eyes scanned the area, glancing across the parked cars and pedestrians walking by, but nothing seemed out of the ordinary. Yet, the foreboding feeling remained.

Gavin quickened his pace, heading toward his car parked just around the corner. He glanced over his shoulder again, his pulse quickening, though he still saw no one suspicious. By the time Gavin reached his car, his nerves were on edge. He unlocked the door and slid into the driver's seat, quickly starting the engine.

As the car purred to life, Gavin took a deep breath, gripping the steering wheel tighter than necessary. He was probably just being paranoid. The city was busy; people were always coming and going. There was no reason for him to feel this way. But the sensation gnawed at him, a constant reminder that something felt... *off*.

He pulled out of the parking spot, merging into the evening traffic as he made his way back to his office. The streets were busy, the headlights of other cars flashing in his mirrors as he weaved through the familiar cityscape. His mind raced as he drove, thinking back to the weekend at the beach, to the laughter with Ashton and the quiet, loving times with Eric. He had everything he could ever want, so why did he feel like his life was unraveling?

Gavin then realized that was such an idiotic and selfish thought. Of course, he knew why. It was all his doing. His affair with Colton was making him feel this way, creating his own *undoing*.

As Gavin reached the office, he parked the car and stepped out, taking another quick glance around before heading inside. The nagging sense that someone was following him lingered, a constant shadow in the back of his mind.

Gavin stepped into the building, the familiar scent of waxed floors and faint coffee filling the air as he made his way through the clean, modern lobby of the real estate office. He was still shaken from the irksome feeling of being watched, but he brushed it off, trying to convince himself that he was just being paranoid. As he approached the elevator, he saw Spencer waving at him from the hallway that led to his office.

"Hey Gavin, got a minute?" Spencer called out, his usual friendly demeanor slightly subdued.

Gavin nodded, his curiosity piqued and changed course toward Spencer's office. Spencer was his boss and friend, someone who rarely sounded serious unless the situation called for it. As he walked down the hall, a knot of anxiety began to form in Gavin's stomach.

"Shut the door, would you?" Spencer said, his voice calm but serious.

Gavin closed the door softly, then took a seat in one of the leather chairs in front of Spencer's desk. "What's going on, Spence?"

Spencer sighed, leaning against his desk, arms folded across his chest. "Listen, I don't mean to alarm you, but something weird has been going on."

Gavin frowned, his anxiety growing. "What do you mean?"

Spencer shifted slightly, his gaze steady. "Some guy's been calling the office. Not just once—he's called multiple times over the past week, asking about you."

Gavin blinked, taken aback. "What? Asking about *me*?"

"Yeah," Spencer confirmed, his tone worrisome. "He asked if I know you, if you work here, and all sorts of personal questions. I didn't give him anything, of course. I wouldn't discuss you with a complete stranger, especially someone who refuses to leave their name."

Gavin's stomach dropped. "Did he say what he wanted?"

"No," Spencer replied, shaking his head. "He was cagey. When I asked who he was or what it was about, he dodged the question. The whole thing felt weird, so I told him I couldn't help him and hung up. But he keeps calling."

Gavin leaned forward, the hairs on the back of his neck rising again. His mind raced back to the strange feeling he'd been having—of being followed, watched. The unease that had been hounding him suddenly felt all too real.

"Do you have any idea who it could be?" Spencer asked, his voice softer now, concern creeping into his tone. "I mean, this guy clearly has a reason to keep asking about you."

Gavin hesitated, his thoughts swirling. "No," he said, his voice strained. "I can't think of anyone. But this is... so bizarre. I've felt like someone's been watching me lately, too."

Spencer's brows furrowed. "Watching you? What do you mean?"

Gavin rubbed his temple, trying to make sense of it all. "It's hard to explain. It's like, whenever I'm out, I just get this feeling like there's someone following me, but I can never spot anyone. I thought maybe it was just in my head, but now..."

Spencer's concern deepened. "That doesn't sound like paranoia. If someone's calling here about you and you've been feeling followed, it could be connected."

Gavin exhaled, leaning back in the chair as the weight of the situation started to settle in. He had been juggling so much—his affair with Colton, his guilt over Eric and Ashton, the pressures of his job—and now this? The tension in his life was becoming unbearable.

"This is the last thing I need," Gavin muttered, rubbing the back of his neck. "Do you think this guy is dangerous?"

Spencer shook his head slightly. "I don't know. The calls weren't threatening, but they were persistent. It's hard to say what his intentions are."

Gavin nodded, his mind racing. "I should've known

something was wrong. I mean, I've been feeling this for a few weeks now."

"*Weeks*?" Spencer repeated, his expression sharpening. "You think it's been happening for that long?"

Gavin sighed. "Yeah. I didn't tell anyone because I thought it was just my guilt. You know, with everything going on, I figured it was all in my head."

Spencer nodded knowingly, his expression softening. "I get it. You've got a lot on your plate. But this—this sounds like something more."

Gavin swallowed hard, his thoughts tumbling over themselves. His secrets, his double life—it felt like everything was starting to cave in. And now, with someone apparently tracking his movements, the walls were closing in faster than he'd expected.

"What should I do?" Gavin asked, his voice tinged with frustration. "I can't just ignore this."

"I'd be cautious," Spencer said, his tone firm. "Keep your eyes open. And if the calls keep coming or if you notice anything else strange, maybe think about getting the police involved."

Gavin nodded, though the thought of involving the authorities made his stomach churn. He couldn't afford for anyone—especially not the police—to start digging into his life. There were too many things he was trying to keep hidden.

Spencer seemed to read his distress, and he softened his tone. "Look, I'm here if you need anything, alright? Whatever's going on, we'll figure it out. Just... don't ignore it."

Gavin met Spencer's gaze, his mind a whirlwind of thoughts and emotions. "Thanks, Spence. I appreciate it."

Spencer gave him a small, reassuring smile, though the tension of the situation in the air lingered. "Just keep your head down, alright? Don't do anything rash."

Gavin nodded, feeling the weight of Spencer's words as he stood to leave. But as he walked out of the office and back toward his own, a new unease settled deep in his chest. Whoever was calling, whoever was following him, they were closing in. And Gavin had no idea what they wanted—or how much they knew.

As he stepped into his office and shut the door behind him, the weight of his secrets pressed down harder than ever. His life was becoming more dangerous, more precarious, and he wasn't sure how much longer he could keep it all from falling apart.

Gavin sat at his desk for thirty minutes after his conversation with his boss, the tension from Spencer's news still gripping him. His thoughts were scattered—flashes of being followed, strange phone calls, and the nagging sense that his life was slipping out of control. His fingers drummed absentmindedly on the surface of his desk, and after a few more minutes of futile attempts to focus, he decided he needed to get out. Sitting in the office wasn't helping.

Gavin quickly gathered his things and decided he would surprise Eric at the hospital. Maybe a gesture of normalcy—something sweet and thoughtful—would help ground him. There was a bakery nearby, a small, charming spot known for its decadent desserts, and he decided to stop there on his way to the hospital. Sharing dessert with Eric and having this connection might calm the storm brewing in his chest.

The air outside was brisk as Gavin stepped onto the sidewalk. The early evening sky was a soft blend of pink and orange as the sun began to set. The bakery wasn't far, just a short walk from his office. As he approached, the warm, buttery scent of freshly baked goods greeted him, and he felt a slight sense of relief wash over him. The display case was filled with an array of beautiful confections—tarts with glossy fruit glazes, decadent chocolate cakes, flaky croissants, and perfectly swirled cupcakes.

He approached the counter, and the friendly woman behind the register offered a warm smile. "What can I get for you today?"

Gavin scanned the case, settling on something simple but rich—Eric's favorite, a decadent chocolate mousse cake with layers of ganache. "I'll take two slices of the chocolate mousse cake," Gavin said, his voice steadier now. "To go."

The woman nodded, carefully packaging the slices into a sleek white box, her movements practiced and precise. "Great choice," she said with a grin. "That one's a best-seller."

Gavin paid and took the box, thanking her as he left the bakery. The walk to the hospital was short, but his mind wandered as he strolled, the weight of everything that had happened recently still pressing down on him. But as the hospital loomed closer, he found himself focusing on Eric—on how much he wanted to just sit with him, talk, and find some sense of balance again.

When he arrived at the hospital, the large, sterile building towering above him, Gavin paused at the entrance. He glanced at the box in his hands, a small, hopeful smile forming on his lips. He could picture Eric's reaction—his eyes lighting up at the sight of the dessert, the warmth of their connection returning, even if just for a moment.

But as Gavin stepped forward, ready to head inside, something caught his eye. Near the side of the building, just out of the flow of foot traffic, he saw two figures standing close together, partially hidden in the shadows. At first, he didn't recognize the other man, but Eric's tall, familiar frame was unmistakable.

Gavin's heart skipped a beat as he stopped in his tracks. Eric was just a few yards away, but he wasn't alone. The two men were close—*too close*. Gavin watched, frozen in place, as Eric leaned in and kissed the man.

Gavin's breath hitched in his throat. The world around him seemed to slow down, the sound of the city fading into the background. He couldn't believe what he was seeing. The man—someone Gavin didn't recognize—returned the kiss, their movements intimate and unhurried. It wasn't just a quick, casual kiss; it was lingering, filled with a familiarity that sent a sharp pang of betrayal through Gavin's chest.

They immediately looked over their shoulders as if checking to ensure no one was watching, guilt flashing across their faces. But instead of pulling away, they shared a quick glance, then turned, walking away together, their shoulders brushing as they strolled down the sidewalk.

Gavin stood there, rooted to the spot, his mind racing. He felt like he had just been punched in the gut. The dessert box felt heavy in his hands, suddenly meaningless, a cruel reminder of how much effort he had put into trying to hold everything together. His vision blurred as tears stung his eyes, but he blinked them back, his mind scrambling to process what he had just seen.

Eric. Kissing someone else.

He wanted to call out, to demand an explanation, to run after them and confront Eric—but the weight of it all was too much. He couldn't face it. Not now. Not like this. Instead, he turned and ran, the sound of his shoes slapping against the pavement barely registering as he fled the scene.

His heart pounded in his chest, his breath coming in ragged gasps as he weaved through the bustling city streets, away from the hospital, away from the truth he had just uncovered. Tears threatened to spill over, but he forced himself to keep moving, not caring where he was going, just needing to escape.

The dessert box clutched in his hand felt ridiculous now, a symbol of everything he thought he was holding onto. He thought back to the weekend at the beach—how perfect it had been, how connected he had felt to Eric. But now it all felt like a lie. Every tender minute, every kiss, every stolen glance—it was all crumbling, and Gavin had no idea how to stop it.

His legs carried him back toward the office, but he didn't have a plan. He just needed to be alone. He needed to think. But more than anything, he needed to process the fact that the life he had been so desperately trying to keep together was falling apart in ways he never anticipated.

And with that, he chucked the dessert box right into the nearest trash bin on the street, hoping that his marriage with Eric would not result in the same way.

Chapter 8

Gavin sat in Dr. Henry Jacobs' office, his body trembling as sobs wracked through him. His hands shook as they gripped the arms of the plush couch, his knuckles turning white from the strain. His world felt like it had shattered, and he was left trying to gather the pieces that seemed to slip through his fingers no matter how hard he tried. The soft, ambient music playing in the background, meant to calm clients, felt distant and meaningless to him now.

The office was the same as it had always been—calming, with soft sage-green walls and warm lighting that bathed the room in a serene glow. The large windows allowed natural light to pour in, casting gentle shadows across the bookshelves lined with psychology textbooks and art that felt intentionally chosen for its abstract ambiguity. A small glass table in the center of the room held a box of tissues and a vase with a single white orchid. The scent of lavender still filled the air, but today, it did nothing to soothe Gavin's frayed nerves.

Dr. Jacobs sat across from him, his expression calm but concerned as he waited patiently for Gavin to regain his composure. The therapist's presence had always been reassuring, a beacon of clarity in the chaos that Gavin's life had become, but today, even Dr. Jacobs couldn't offer the solace Gavin so desperately needed.

"What's the emergency, Gavin?" Dr. Jacobs asked, his voice soft but direct. He broke the silence with a familiar tone that made it clear this was a safe space.

Gavin wiped his face, his cheeks wet with tears, and struggled to catch his breath. "It's Eric," he finally choked out, his voice raw and shaky. "He's having an affair. I—I saw him. I saw him kissing someone else outside the hospital."

Dr. Jacobs leaned forward slightly, his brow furrowed. "I see," he said, his voice calm but probing. "So, it's okay for you, but not for him?"

The question hit Gavin like a punch to the gut, and his breath hitched again. "Ugh!" he groaned, covering his face with his hands. "I know it's wrong. I know what I've been doing with Colton is wrong. But at least I know what Colton is about! I know he's not someone I could ever have a real relationship with. It's different with Eric."

Dr. Jacobs waited, letting the silence stretch just long enough for Gavin to speak again.

"What if Eric's in love with this guy? What if he leaves me?" Gavin's voice cracked as his hands dropped into his lap, and he looked at Dr. Jacobs with desperation in his eyes. "What if… what if there's something wrong with me? What if I've been so focused on my own mistakes that I didn't even see this coming?"

Dr. Jacobs sighed softly, sitting back in his chair. "You're overwhelmed right now, Gavin. It's a lot to process. But let's start with what you're feeling. You're afraid Eric might be in love with this man?"

Gavin nodded, biting his lip as another wave of emotion threatened to overwhelm him. "Yes! I mean… I don't know! I didn't think Eric would ever do something like this. He's always been so perfect. So loving and attentive. And now I don't know what to think." He paused, then added, "and what does that say about me? I've been the one who's been lying and cheating this whole time, and now… *this*."

Dr. Jacobs studied him, his fingers steepled beneath his chin. "You've been having an affair with Colton for some time now, and I know you've struggled with guilt. But let's ask a difficult question—why does it hurt so much to think that Eric might be doing the same?"

Gavin's breath hitched again, his chest tight as he tried

to find the right words. "Because... because I love him. And this isn't just about some physical thing. What if this means more? What if Eric's been unhappy, and I didn't see it? What if he's been pulling away, and I've been so caught up in my own mess that I didn't notice? He's never given me any reason to think he'd cheat, and yet... I saw them. I saw *him*."

Dr. Jacobs remained quiet before speaking gently. "You've said before that Colton provides something different for you. Something wild and captivating that you don't get from Eric. Do you think Eric is seeking something similar from this other man?"

Gavin shook his head vigorously, his voice rising slightly. "No. Eric isn't like that. He's... *perfect*. He's been loving, doting, and... better than ever. Things have been amazing between us recently. We just had a weekend at the beach, and it was perfect. We were laughing, holding hands, kissing under the stars. He's been more romantic than he's been in years."

Dr. Jacobs arched an eyebrow, his expression curious. "So, things have been better than ever between you two?"

Gavin nodded, his throat tightening as more tears threatened to spill. "Yes, better than ever."

Dr. Jacobs tapped his fingers against his knee thoughtfully before leaning in slightly. "Then it's not about him pulling away. So, let me ask you this—why did you get involved with Colton in the first place? If things were so good between you and Eric, why did you feel the need to seek something outside your marriage?"

Gavin squeezed his eyes shut, his mind racing through the events that had led him to this point. "I don't know," he whispered, but he knew that wasn't true even as he said the words. Gavin did know. He just didn't want to admit it.

Dr. Jacobs waited, his gaze steady. "Be honest with yourself, Gavin. You came here because you said you wanted to save your marriage. If that's true, you need to understand why you stepped outside of it in the first place."

Gavin's hands trembled in his lap as he forced himself to speak. "Because… because it was exciting," he admitted, his voice barely above a whisper. "Colton was different. He made me feel… *free*, I guess. Like I wasn't just a husband and a father. He made me feel alive in a way that I hadn't felt in a long time. And I thought… I thought I could keep it separate. That it wouldn't hurt anyone."

Dr. Jacobs nodded slowly, his expression thoughtful. "But it has hurt you. It's hurt your family, even if they don't know it yet. And now, seeing Eric with someone else, you're realizing just how fragile everything is."

Gavin nodded, his chest heaving with emotion. "I want to save my marriage, Dr. Jacobs. I don't want to lose Eric. I love him. I can't lose him."

Dr. Jacobs leaned forward, his voice soft but firm. "If you want to save your marriage, Gavin, you're going to have to be completely honest and not just with me, but with Eric—and more importantly, with yourself. You can't keep living in two worlds. You have to decide what you want, and you have to decide if you're ready to face the consequences of your actions."

Gavin swallowed hard, the truth sinking in. "I know," he whispered. "I know I can't keep doing this. But I'm scared. I'm scared of what's going to happen."

Dr. Jacobs' expression softened, and he gave Gavin a reassuring nod. "It's okay to be scared, Gavin. But if you're serious about saving your marriage, you have to start somewhere. And that somewhere is with the truth."

Gavin wiped his face with the back of his hand, his mind still spinning. But deep down, he knew Dr. Jacobs was right. He had been running from the truth for far too long, and now it was time to face it, no matter how painful it might be.

For a few seconds, Gavin reflected on what Dr. Jacobs

was saying. He sat back in the therapist's chair, his hands clenched together in his lap. Gavin's heart pounded in his chest, and he stared down at his feet, unable to meet Dr. Jacobs' gaze. His eyes were still red from the earlier crying, but the torrent of emotions swirling inside him had yet to settle.

Dr. Jacobs broke the silence first, his voice quiet but firm. "Gavin," he continued, leaning forward slightly, "do you think there's a possibility that Eric knows about you and Colton?"

The question hung in the air, and for an instance, Gavin felt as though the ground had fallen out from under him. His pulse quickened, and he blinked, trying to process the possibility.

Eric knowing? Could it be? He'd been so careful—or so he thought.

"It's interesting you say that," Gavin replied after a long pause, his voice low. He ran a hand through his hair, trying to shake the disturbing feeling that had been tormenting him for weeks. "I can't shake the feeling that I'm being followed. It's like someone's always watching me. I've felt it for weeks now. And then there's Spencer…" Gavin trailed off, recalling the conversation with his boss. "Spencer says someone keeps calling the office and asking questions about me. Like whether I work there or if he knows me. It's weird."

Dr. Jacobs nodded, his expression thoughtful. "And what are you doing about it?"

Gavin let out a bitter laugh, shaking his head as he slumped back in the chair. "What do you suggest I do? Call the police and say, 'Hey, I'm having an affair, and I think my husband's hired someone to follow me and confirm it?' Sounds like a great plan."

Dr. Jacobs didn't react to Gavin's sarcasm. Instead, he leaned forward, his gaze piercing. "Gavin, what did you think was going to happen when you started this affair? You had to have seen some kind of end picture in mind. What was it? What did you expect to happen after all of this?"

Gavin swallowed hard, his mouth dry. He had no honest answer to that. What had he been thinking when he got involved with Colton? In those early days, it had felt simple—a thrilling, secret escape from the pressures of his life. But now, with everything spiraling out of control, the consequences of his choices loomed larger than ever before.

"Not this," Gavin muttered, his voice barely above a whisper. "For sure, not this."

Dr. Jacobs sighed, tapping his fingers lightly against his chair. "Gavin, I know this isn't what you expected. But let's be honest—you didn't really expect anything, did you? You were so caught up in the rush and escape that you didn't think about where it would lead. But now you're here, and things are spiraling. You can spin it however you want, but the fact remains—you've been having an affair, and you knew there would be a fallout, eventually. *This* is that fallout."

Gavin winced at the words, feeling their weight sink into him. He had spent so much time justifying his actions to himself, convincing himself that he could compartmentalize his life, that he could keep Colton and Eric separate. But now, faced with the reality that Eric might know about his affair and that someone might be watching his every move, the walls continued to close in.

"How am I supposed to deal with it?" Gavin asked, his voice breaking with vexation. "I feel like everything is slipping away. Eric, Ashton, my career—it's all falling apart. And I don't know what to do. I didn't mean for any of this to happen."

Dr. Jacobs met his eyes, his expression softening slightly. "I understand that you're scared, Gavin. But denial isn't going to fix this. What you need to do now is figure out what you want. Do you want to save your marriage? If you do, you have to confront this. You have to be honest with Eric. You can't keep running from the truth."

Gavin felt tears welling up again, his throat tightening. "I don't want to lose him. I don't want to lose my family. I love Eric. I really do. But I've screwed everything up so badly. I don't even know if he'll listen to me."

"You have to give him the chance to listen," Dr. Jacobs said gently. "But you also have to be prepared for the fact that he might not. He may already know more than you think. The calls to Spencer, the feeling of being followed—that's not just paranoia, Gavin. Something is happening, and the longer you wait, the more control you lose over the situation."

Gavin ran his hands over his face, overwhelmed by the truth of Dr. Jacobs' words. He had been trying to hold on to both worlds—his life with Eric and his affair with Colton—and now it was all slipping through his fingers.

"I never wanted to hurt him," Gavin whispered, tears spilling over. "I never wanted to hurt anyone."

Dr. Jacobs watched him, then spoke, his tone calm but firm. "I believe that. But now, you have to deal with the consequences of your actions. You need to be honest with yourself and with Eric. Otherwise, this is only going to get worse."

Gavin nodded weakly, the weight of it all pressing down on him. He had no idea how he was going to approach Eric, no idea what he would even say. But one thing was clear—he couldn't keep running from the truth. It was time to face it, no matter how terrifying it might be.

The session ended quietly, with Dr. Jacobs reminding him to take things one step at a time. But as Gavin left the office, his mind raced with fear and uncertainty. He knew what he had to do, but the thought of confronting Eric, of potentially losing everything he loved, was almost unbearable.

As he stepped outside into the fading evening light, Gavin took a deep breath, trying to steady his nerves. The brisk air bit at his skin, but it wasn't enough to clear his mind. He knew he couldn't put it off any longer. It was time to face the consequences of his actions and deal with the truth—no matter where it led. But before handling Eric, there was something else he needed to do. So, he decided that first he would deal with Colton.

Chapter 9

Gavin stared at his phone for a while before he finally hit dial. His heart raced, knowing what needed to be done, but that didn't make it any easier. He'd been avoiding this conversation for too long, letting things spiral out of control. Now, with everything crashing down around him, he knew he couldn't keep stringing Colton along. It wasn't fair to either of them, and more importantly, it wasn't fair to Eric or Ashton.

The phone rang twice before Colton's familiar voice came through, casual and amused. "Hey sexy. What's going on? I didn't expect to hear from you this soon."

Gavin swallowed hard. "We need to talk. Can you meet me? There's a place in the next town over, a restaurant. It's quiet. We won't be seen."

Colton paused, the amusement in his voice fading slightly. "Sure, but why all the secrecy? What's going on?"

"I'll explain when we meet," Gavin replied, his voice tight. "It's important. Just... just meet me there."

The line went quiet for a second before Colton sighed. "Alright. Text me the address. I'll be there."

They agreed to meet at a small, tucked-away restaurant in the neighboring town. It was a place Gavin had chosen specifically because it was far enough away from anyone who might recognize him in public. When he arrived, the restaurant was dimly lit, its interior intimate and rustic. Dark wooden tables were scattered throughout the room, lit by small candles that cast a soft glow. The scent of grilled meats and herbs filled the air, blending with the faint sound of clinking glasses and low whispers of conversation from other diners.

Gavin took a deep breath, stepping inside and scanning the room until he saw Colton already seated in a corner booth near the back. Colton looked as effortlessly attractive as ever—dressed in a simple white shirt that fit him just right, his dark hair slightly tousled in that careless way that always made Gavin's heart race. But today, the usual excitement Gavin felt when seeing Colton was replaced by a heavy sense of dread.

Gavin approached the table, and Colton flashed him a smile. "There you are," he said, raising a glass of wine to his lips. "What's this about, then?"

Gavin slid into the booth, his stomach churning. A waiter approached, and they quickly ordered a bottle of red wine and two entrees, though Gavin barely registered what he asked for. His mind was already racing with what he needed to say.

They sat in silence after the waiter left, Colton sipping his wine and watching Gavin with a curious expression. Finally, Gavin couldn't take it anymore. "Colton," he began, his voice trembling slightly, "we need to end this."

Colton raised an eyebrow, his lips still curved in that faint smile. "End what, exactly?"

"*Us*," Gavin said, feeling a lump rise in his throat. "I can't keep doing this. My life is falling apart, and I can't handle it anymore."

Colton leaned back in the booth, his smile fading into something colder, more serious. "And not seeing me is going to make that easier?"

Gavin nodded, swallowing hard. "It's my only option. I have to fix things with Eric. I have to focus on my family. This—" he gestured between them, "—it's tearing me apart. I can't live with this guilt anymore."

Colton's expression hardened, and he let out a bitter laugh. "So that's it? You think cutting me off is going to solve all your problems?"

Gavin clenched his fists under the table, trying to keep his voice steady. "It's not that simple. I need to try and salvage what I can. Eric—he doesn't deserve this. Ashton doesn't deserve this, either. I've made a mess of everything."

Colton leaned forward, his eyes narrowing. "Is that why you wanted to meet here in public? So I couldn't make a scene? So I couldn't wrap you in my arms and sway you the right way, like I've always been able to do?" His voice dropped, filled with an edge of seduction. "You know you turn me on so much. It's not going to be easy to let this go between us."

Gavin's breath hitched at the heat in Colton's words, but he forced himself to push past it. "I can't do it anymore," he repeated, his voice firmer now. "This is the only way. It's over."

Colton's eyes flashed with anger and hurt. "I know I'm not the nicest guy in the world," he said, his voice low and bitter, "but this is a real shitty way to end things. After everything we've been through."

Gavin felt the weight of Colton's words, guilt surging up inside him. "I know," he said quietly. "But I don't have a choice. I can't keep doing this. You have to understand."

Colton stood up abruptly, shaking his head. "No, Gavin. I understand perfectly. I just hate the way you went about doing it." His voice was tight with emotion, and for an instance, Gavin saw a flash of vulnerability in Colton's eyes—something rare and raw. Without another word, Colton turned and stormed out of the restaurant, leaving Gavin sitting alone in the booth.

Gavin watched him go, his heart pounding and his chest tight. The wine in front of him sat untouched, but he reached for the glass now, his hands trembling as he took a long, slow sip. The bitter taste of the wine did little to ease the weight pressing down on him.

He stared at the half-eaten meal in front of him, unable to summon any appetite. The restaurant felt darker now, more oppressive, as if the walls were closing in around him. He had done what he needed to do, but instead of relief, all he felt was a deep, aching sense of loss.

As he sat there, trying to process the whirlwind of emotions swirling inside him, his eyes wandered around the restaurant. That's when he saw it—a man at the bar, his phone aimed directly at him, as if he were taking a picture.

Gavin's heart lurched. "Hey!" he shouted, standing up abruptly from the booth. But the man at the bar didn't wait. He quickly slipped off the stool and darted out of the restaurant, disappearing into the busy street outside.

Gavin ran after him, bursting through the doors and onto the sidewalk, his heart racing with panic. He scanned the crowd, searching for any sign of the man, but it was no use. The street was crowded, and the man had already vanished, lost in the sea of people.

Gavin's breath came in short, sharp bursts as he stood there, his eyes wild and his mind racing. Someone had been watching him. Someone had followed him here. His worst fear was becoming a reality.

Eventually, he soon forced himself to calm down. He couldn't stay here any longer. He had to get out, to regroup and figure out what was happening. He turned and walked back into the restaurant, his legs feeling weak beneath him. The waiter glanced at him curiously, but Gavin simply reached into his wallet, threw some cash onto the table to cover the bill, and left.

As he stepped back out into the city streets, the feeling of being watched clung to him like a shadow, and Gavin knew he was in deeper trouble than he had ever imagined.

The bar was dimly lit, casting warm, amber hues across the dark wooden floors and brick walls. The atmosphere droned with quiet conversation, the clink of glasses, and the low strum of blues music playing from the speakers above. It was the kind of place where people came to disappear, where no one asked questions, and no one cared enough to listen to your answers. The large, U-shaped bar was lined with patrons, hunched over their drinks, bathed in the golden light from the hanging Edison bulbs. A haze of cigarette smoke lingered near the back, where a few people were gathered around a pool table, laughing in hushed tones.

A guy in jeans and a black leather jacket—short, stocky, and with a perpetual five o'clock shadow—sat at the bar, swirling the melting ice in his whiskey glass. His leather jacket creaked with every movement, but he remained completely furtive in a cap pulled low over his brow. His phone sat on the bar next to him, the screen still illuminated with a series of photos he'd taken earlier that day of Gavin. He glanced up when a tall man entered the bar, scanning the room before locking eyes with him.

Wesley.

Wesley was hard to miss. He had the kind of presence that turned heads—tall, broad-shouldered, with a neatly trimmed beard and intense, calculating eyes. He moved through the bar with the ease of someone who belonged, his tailored brown coat swishing slightly as he approached the man in the black leather jacket, who was actually a private investigator he had hired. He sat down on the stool next to him.

Wesley didn't waste time with pleasantries. With a quick nod, he flagged down the bartender and ordered a neat bourbon. The bartender moved swiftly, and soon, Wesley had the glass in hand, the amber liquid catching the light as he took a long, deliberate sip.

"Alright," Wesley said, his voice low and gravelly.

"What've you got for me?"

The P.I. leaned back in his stool, lifting his whiskey glass lazily before taking a sip. "He's a real estate agent. Married. Got a kid, about eight years old, I'd say. From what I've seen, he's pretty normal. Works the nine-to-five grind at an office unless he is out selling homes and goes to baseball games with the kid—nothing out of the ordinary."

Wesley's gaze narrowed as he studied the man. "And?"

The private investigator smirked, setting his glass down and reaching for his phone. "And... I think he's got himself a side-piece boyfriend. Saw them together at a restaurant today." He tapped on his phone, pulling up a series of photos—grainy, taken from a distance, but clear enough to tell the story. "It looked like he ended things with the guy, though. They had dinner and some wine, and then the guy stormed out. Couldn't hear the conversation, but you could see it all over their faces. Shit was tense."

Wesley grabbed the phone, his thumb swiping through the photos one by one. Each shot showed Gavin sitting across from Colton in the dimly lit restaurant, their faces strained with emotion. There was no mistaking the look of someone breaking off a relationship. Wesley frowned, his brow furrowing deeper with each photo.

"This doesn't sound like him at all," Wesley muttered under his breath, though the P.I. heard it clearly.

The private investigator took another sip of his whiskey, glancing sideways at Wesley. "Then what do you think? Do I have the wrong guy?"

Wesley shook his head slowly, his eyes still fixed on the photos. "Nope. The pictures don't lie. You definitely have him. That's Gavin, alright."

The P.I. raised an eyebrow, curiosity piqued. "It's none of my business," he said, his tone casual but laced with curiosity. "But who is he to you? What's the deal with this guy?"

Wesley's jaw tightened, and he downed the rest of his bourbon in one swift motion, setting the glass down with a soft clink. He let the question hang in the air before answering, his voice low and laced with bitterness.

"He ruined my fucking life."

Chapter 10

The school auditorium was dimly lit, its rows of seats filled with parents and families eagerly waiting to watch their children perform on stage. The faint scent of old wood and the muffled sound of instruments warming up backstage gave the space an air of familiarity that reminded Gavin of his own childhood school recitals. He arrived a little late, slipping through the double doors as quietly as he could, careful not to draw attention as he stepped into the back of the room.

He scanned the audience, his heart already heavy from the weight of everything that had been happening. His eyes immediately found Eric seated up near the front, his posture perfect as always, watching the stage with quiet focus. Eric's presence was magnetic, even in something as mundane as a school recital. He wore a simple, dark blazer, his hair neatly combed, the perfect picture of a devoted husband and father.

Gavin considered walking up the aisle to sit beside him, but the thought of making a scene during Ashton's performance stopped him. He didn't want to interrupt or draw any unnecessary attention, not tonight. Tonight was about Ashton, and despite everything weighing on his mind, Gavin's heart swelled with pride as his eyes landed on his son, seated among the other children on stage, trumpet in hand as they came out from behind the curtains.

Ashton, dressed in the school's formal black-and-white performance attire, looked so focused, his small hands gripping the trumpet tightly. His face was serious and concentrated as he sat among his peers, waiting for his cue to play. The stage lights illuminated his face, casting a soft glow on his determined expression.

Gavin's heart ached with how much he loved his son. Ashton was growing up so fast, and it pained Gavin to think of the world of adult problems that loomed over their family—the secrets, the lies, the betrayals.

Ashton didn't deserve this, Gavin thought, watching his son with a mixture of pride and sorrow. He didn't deserve the drama, the affairs, the mess that Gavin had created. No, Ashton deserved a happy family, one that wasn't fractured by deceit.

The soft sound of instruments tuning came to an end, and the conductor raised his baton. The recital began, and the children launched into their first piece. The music filled the room, a mixture of trumpets, violins, and flutes blending together. Gavin's eyes never left Ashton, watching his son hit the notes with precision, his face filled with pride and focus.

I can fix this, Gavin thought to himself as he stood quietly in the back of the room, his arms crossed over his chest. The music flowed around him, but his mind was racing with resolve. *I have to fix this. Eric and I—we can get through this. We have to, for Ashton's sake.*

As Eric sat near the front, oblivious to Gavin's presence, his eyes locked on Ashton as well. There was no doubt in Gavin's mind that Eric loved their son as much as he did. And if Eric still cared about their family, they could rebuild from the wreckage. *It's not too late*, Gavin thought. *We can still fix this.*

The music swelled, the final notes of the song hanging in the air before the room erupted in applause. The children on stage beamed, proud of their performance, and Gavin clapped along with the rest of the audience. Ashton's face lit up with a broad smile as he put his trumpet down, looking out over the crowd, his eyes searching for his dads. Gavin's heart clenched when Ashton's gaze lingered before he looked away, unable to find his father among the sea of faces.

As the applause died down, the music teacher, a tall man with dark hair and an easy smile, stepped onto the stage. He raised a hand to quiet the room, his voice clear and warm as he addressed the audience. "Thank you, everyone, for coming tonight and supporting these wonderful students. They've worked so hard, and I couldn't be prouder of all their accomplishments."

Gavin's stomach dropped.

It was him.

The music teacher—the man standing up on stage, charming the crowd—was the same man Gavin had seen Eric kissing outside the hospital.

His breath caught in his throat as the realization hit him like a punch to the gut. The man who had been sleeping with his husband was standing right there, in front of all these parents, thanking them for attending the recital, and Gavin had never even known. The man was well-groomed, with a casual yet professional presence, his dark hair neatly styled and his clothes perfectly tailored. His smile was genuine, and the audience clapped politely as he finished speaking.

But what sent a fresh wave of nausea through Gavin was what happened next.

The music teacher, still standing at the edge of the stage, glanced toward the front row, where Eric was seated. A small, knowing smile crossed the teacher's lips, and then—Gavin's heart nearly stopped—he *winked*.

A slow, casual wink accompanied by an unmistakable smirk.

Gavin's blood ran cold. He stood frozen in place, the sound of clapping around him becoming distant, muffled, as though he were underwater. The teacher's smirk lingered for just a moment longer, and then his eyes shifted away back to the crowd as if nothing had happened.

But Gavin had seen it. He had *felt* it.

The rest of the world faded, and all that remained was the crushing weight of betrayal. The man who had been smiling warmly at the audience, who had been guiding and teaching his son, was the same man who had shattered Gavin's marriage. And Eric—Eric had been sitting there the entire time, knowing. *Watching*.

Gavin's resolve, the strength he'd felt only seconds before, crumbled instantly. His heart felt like it had been ripped from his chest. He couldn't think, couldn't move. The weight of it all—the lies, the infidelity, the realization that his life had spiraled out of control—pressed down on him, suffocating him.

The applause finally subsided, and parents began to stand, chatting among themselves, moving toward the exit. Gavin stood still, rooted in place, watching Eric rise from his seat, oblivious to the storm raging inside his husband. Eric smiled at someone nearby with his usual composed self, but to Gavin, it all felt like a sick joke.

Gavin couldn't do it anymore. He couldn't stand there, watching the man who had betrayed him, watching the man who had torn their family apart, smirk at his husband from the stage. Without thinking, Gavin turned and slipped out of the auditorium, his chest tight, his mind a whirlwind of pain and disbelief.

He needed air. He needed to escape.

But most of all, he needed to figure out how he was ever going to confront the truth that was now staring him in the face.

As the doors to the auditorium closed behind him, the sounds of the recital faded, leaving only the echo of Gavin's shattered world.

Gavin sat in the familiar chair in Dr. Henry Jacobs' office, his body slumped forward, arms resting on his knees. He was fidgeting—a constant, nervous energy vibrating under his skin as his foot tapped against the floor. His face was pale, his eyes bloodshot from sleepless nights and the stress that had been gnawing at him for what felt like an eternity. His usually crisp shirt was wrinkled, and his hands kept running through his hair as if trying to smooth out his disheveled thoughts.

Dr. Jacobs sat across from him, the serene calm of his office a stark contrast to the emotional storm swirling inside Gavin. The warm, earthy tones of the walls and the soft light streaming in from the large windows were meant to soothe, but today, the peaceful environment only magnified Gavin's inner chaos. He stared blankly out the window, his gaze distant, lost in the jumble of images and memories from the recital—the music, Ashton's smiling face, and that wink.

That damn wink.

"He's a teacher at the school, for Christ's sake!" Gavin blurted out suddenly, his voice cracking. He sat up straighter, his hands clenched into fists on his knees. "I saw the way he smiled and winked at Eric in the audience. It wasn't just some casual glance. It was… it was like they were sharing some private joke. They acted like I wasn't even there."

Dr. Jacobs studied Gavin, his eyes narrowing slightly as he folded his hands in his lap. His posture was relaxed, but there was an edge to his tone when he finally spoke. "Gavin," he began slowly, "is it possible that maybe you're imagining some of this? You've been under a lot of stress lately. Could it be that you're seeing something that isn't really there?"

Gavin's head snapped toward Dr. Jacobs, disbelief etched on his face. "What? No. It's not possible. I *know* what I saw." His voice rose slightly, defensive, as if daring Dr. Jacobs to question his sanity. "I saw the way they looked at each other. It wasn't some… friendly smile. There's something going on between them. I saw that kiss at the hospital, but there's something more. I can feel it."

Dr. Jacobs nodded, his expression neutral, but his eyes remained sharp, searching Gavin's face for any trace of doubt. "Alright. So, if you're certain, what are you going to do about it? Are you going to confront him?"

Gavin leaned back in the chair, releasing a long, exasperated breath. His hands ran over his face, and he shook his head slowly. "I don't know. Maybe. I haven't even had time to process it yet. I just keep thinking… what if I confront him and he tells me he doesn't love me anymore? What if he tells me he loves this… this *guy* instead? What if he leaves me? What am I supposed to do then?"

His voice cracked again at the end, and he threw his hands up in the air, frustration and helplessness swirling together in a bitter cocktail of emotions.

Dr. Jacobs sat up a little straighter, his gaze never leaving Gavin's. "I want you to keep going with this," he said, his voice firmer now. "Ask yourself all of those questions you're afraid of. Don't stop. Work with me here, Gavin. Let's go through it."

Gavin stared at Dr. Jacobs, his brow furrowed in confusion. "What do you mean? Go through what?"

"All the questions," Dr. Jacobs replied. "The ones you're terrified to ask. What's going on in your head right now? What if Eric tells you he loves this man? What if he leaves you? You need to confront those fears, not hide from them. And while you're at it, ask the other questions, too. Ask yourself how long this has been going on. Is this new? Has he been seeing this man behind your back for months, maybe even years? How often do *you* even see Eric lately? How often do you feel like you're actually connected?"

Gavin looked down at his hands, his stomach twisting as Dr. Jacobs' words cut deep. He didn't want to confront these questions, but knew he had to. Slowly, almost reluctantly, he spoke. "We've been distant, I guess. But it's not like we're strangers. We still talk, we still... I mean, the weekend at the beach was amazing. He's been romantic and loving. It's not like he's pulled away."

Dr. Jacobs nodded. "And yet, here you are, doubting everything. What does that tell you?"

Gavin's eyes flashed with a mix of anger and hurt. "It tells me that I'm losing him. It tells me that I've screwed everything up so badly that maybe Eric's just... over it. Maybe he's bored with me. Maybe this other guy is everything I'm not."

"Is that what you think?" Dr. Jacobs pressed, his voice calm but unrelenting. "That Eric's bored with you?"

Gavin clenched his fists again, his jaw tight. "I don't know! Maybe! I mean, why else would he be doing this? I haven't been perfect, but I've been trying, especially recently. But if he's already checked out... if he's already got someone else—"

"Stop," Dr. Jacobs interrupted, his voice firm. "You're getting too far ahead of yourself. And this isn't about what Eric might be thinking or feeling. This is about *you* right now, Gavin. I need you to focus on *you*. Are you going to talk to Eric? Are you going to confront him about what you saw?"

Gavin leaned forward, resting his elbows on his knees as he buried his face in his hands, breathing deeply, trying to calm the storm inside. "I don't know if I can," he finally admitted, his voice muffled by his hands. "What if I'm wrong? What if I confront him, and it all blows up in my face?"

Dr. Jacobs leaned back, his eyes softening just slightly. "You can't keep running from this, Gavin. You've been avoiding the truth for a long time now—whether it's about your affair with Colton or Eric's possible affair with this man. If you want to save your marriage, you need to face the truth. No matter how painful it is."

Gavin's hands fell away from his face, and he looked

up at Dr. Jacobs, his eyes filled with a mixture of fear and determination. "I just don't know if I can handle the truth," he whispered, his voice barely audible. "What if the truth is that it's already too late?"

Dr. Jacobs went quiet before he spoke again, his voice gentle but firm. "That's a risk you have to take, but avoiding it will only make things worse. You need to be honest with Eric. You need to be honest with yourself. Whatever happens, you'll deal with it. But right now, you're living in fear of the unknown. That's no way to live."

Gavin nodded slowly, the weight of Dr. Jacobs' words settling over him like a heavy blanket. He knew his therapist was right, but the thought of confronting Eric, of opening the door to whatever truth lay behind it, was terrifying.

"I'll think about it," Gavin said softly, his voice cracking.

Dr. Jacobs gave him a small, understanding nod. "That's all I'm asking. Take the time you need, but don't avoid it forever. The longer you wait, the harder it will be."

Gavin leaned back in the chair, staring out the window once more. The world outside seemed so calm, so normal, but inside, everything felt like it was crumbling.

He began to have second thoughts about all of this, coming here to spill his heart out to Dr. Jacobs. Was he being weak by doing this? Couldn't he handle all of this on his own? He should be able to. A strong person wouldn't need to depend on anyone else to help get them through this.

Finally, he snapped. "What is the point of this!?" Gavin's voice rang out, filled with impatience and desperation. He couldn't take it anymore. The questions, the probing, the relentless search for answers he didn't want to face. He just wanted it to stop.

Dr. Jacobs leaned back slightly in his chair, his expression calm but firm. "Oh, come on, Gavin," he replied, his voice steady but challenging. "You know exactly what the point of this is."

Gavin threw his hands up in the air, exasperated. "Ugh! I don't want to do this!" His voice cracked as he spoke, his agitation palpable. He was tired, emotionally drained, and the idea of continuing to dig deeper into his pain felt unbearable.

Dr. Jacobs didn't flinch. "Say the words, Gavin. Let's get to the root of it. Tell *him*."

Gavin's eyes flickered with rage as he glared at Dr. Jacobs. "Fine. Fine! I'll do it. I'll say it out loud. Why is he doing this to me, huh? Why?" His voice was sharp, laced with bitterness and confusion. "What did I do wrong? Why is *Eric* treating me like I don't matter? Like I'm nothing to him?"

Dr. Jacobs sat up a little straighter, his eyes focused on Gavin's, unwavering. "No, Gavin. Don't ask me. Ask *him*. Ask it out loud to Eric. Come on. You can do it."

Gavin's face twisted in pain, and he shook his head, the words catching in his throat. "No! I… I seriously don't want to hear the answers. I can't—I can't bear it. What if he says I don't mean anything to him anymore? What if he says he's in love with this other guy?" His voice broke as the weight of his fear spilled out. "It's like… he's treating me like I mean nothing to him."

The room was heavy with silence as Gavin's words lingered in the air. He was shaking now, his fury dissolving into something more fragile—something that had been buried deep for years.

Dr. Jacobs watched him carefully, his voice softer now. "That must feel terrible."

Gavin's face crumpled, the dam of his emotions finally breaking. Tears spilled over, and he wiped them away angrily with the back of his hand as if he were ashamed of them. He tried to speak, but couldn't get the words out. His chest heaved with the effort to keep from falling apart completely.

"I'm used to it," Gavin whispered after a long pause, his voice barely audible.

Dr. Jacobs frowned slightly, leaning forward, his eyes

filled with concern. "What do you mean, Gavin?"

Gavin sniffed, staring at the floor again, his fingers digging into the armrests of the chair. He didn't want to talk about it. He hadn't talked about it in years, but it was there, lurking in the background of everything—the reason he had always felt like he was holding on by a thread. The reason why he was terrified of being abandoned.

"My family," Gavin began, his voice flat, almost emotionless now. "They were... they were never there for me. Not in the way families are supposed to be." His words came out in short bursts, each one filled with pain he had long since buried.

Dr. Jacobs remained silent, giving Gavin the space to continue.

"My mom..." Gavin paused, swallowing hard as he tried to push the memories away. "She wasn't... *well*. Mentally, I mean. She was always in and out of hospitals, or rather, psychiatric wards, never stable. I never knew if she was going to be there when I came home from school or if she was going to be... gone again."

Gavin's eyes were distant, staring at something only he could see, lost in the past. "And one day, years later, my dad... he left. He couldn't handle it. One day, he just packed up and walked out. I was only twelve at the time."

Dr. Jacobs nodded slightly, his expression compassionate but reserved, waiting for Gavin to open up more.

"There was no one else," Gavin continued, his voice bitter now. "No extended family, no one who cared. I spent most of my teenage years in foster homes and even on the streets, bouncing around from one place to another. Nobody wanted me. Nobody stayed."

His voice grew quieter, more vulnerable. "I learned pretty early on that people leave, that no one sticks around. I was always the problem, the one who was too much to deal with."

Gavin stopped, his breath shaky as the memories overwhelmed him. He hadn't talked about this in years. He had locked it away, pretending that it didn't matter, that it hadn't shaped who he was. But now, sitting in Dr. Jacobs' office, it all came rushing back—the abandonment, the loneliness, the feeling of never being good enough.

"And now Eric's doing the same thing," Gavin whispered, his voice cracking again. "I thought... I thought he was different. But maybe I was wrong. Maybe I just don't know how to keep people around. Maybe I'm destined to be left behind."

Dr. Jacobs leaned forward, his eyes filled with empathy. "Gavin, listen to me. This is not about you being unworthy or unlovable. What you went through as a child—no one should have to go through that. But you need to separate your past from what's happening now. You're not that kid anymore. You're not powerless. You can have control over your life and your relationships. But you need to confront what's happening. You need to confront Eric, not avoid it because you're afraid of reliving that pain."

Gavin wiped at his eyes again, trying to pull himself together. He felt exhausted and emotionally drained, but the weight of the truth settled over him like a heavy blanket. He had spent his whole life running from the fear of being abandoned and unloved. And now, it was happening again—or at least, he feared it was.

"I don't want to lose him," Gavin said softly, his voice shaking. "I don't want to lose my family."

Dr. Jacobs nodded, his voice gentle but firm. "Then you have to fight for it, Gavin. But that starts with being honest. With yourself and with Eric. You can't avoid it any longer."

Gavin nodded weakly, knowing that the real battle was just beginning. He wasn't sure if he had the strength to face it, but he knew he no longer had a choice.

The truth was waiting for him, whether he liked it or not.

Chapter 11

Gavin sat in his car, the engine idling quietly as he stared through the windshield at Ashton's school. His hands gripped the steering wheel tightly, knuckles turning white as his mind raced. Ashton's music teacher—Mr. Bringham, or rather, *Jason Bringham*, was the man who had so casually winked at Eric during the school recital. The man who had been sleeping with his husband, destroying their marriage right under his nose. Gavin's jaw clenched at the thought. He knew he couldn't confront Eric yet, not without solid proof. But to get that proof, he needed to dig deeper. He needed to learn more about Jason Bringham.

It was time to follow him.

Gavin's eyes locked onto the school entrance, his heart pounding in his chest as he waited. The school day had just ended, and students were beginning to trickle out, backpacks slung over their shoulders as they made their way to waiting cars or buses. He knew Jason would be finishing up soon. Gavin had carefully planned this, making sure his work schedule was clear so he could tail Jason without raising suspicion.

After what felt like an eternity, Gavin spotted Jason walking out of the building. The music teacher looked as calm and composed as ever, his hair neatly styled, a casual jacket thrown over his shoulders. He moved with an air of confidence that only added to Gavin's simmering anger. How long had Jason been deceiving him? How long had he been sleeping with Eric while smiling at Gavin during school recitals?

Gavin gritted his teeth and watched Jason cross the parking lot, heading toward his car. Gavin's pulse quickened.

Now was his chance.

As soon as Jason got into his dark red sedan, Gavin pulled out of his parking spot and began to follow, keeping a safe distance so he wouldn't be noticed.

The drive across the city was tense, Gavin's eyes darting between Jason's car and the road ahead. He couldn't afford to lose him, but he also didn't want to risk being spotted. The sun hung low in the sky, casting long shadows across the buildings as they wound through the city streets. Jason seemed completely unaware he was being followed, his car moving steadily through the light evening traffic.

After about fifteen minutes, Jason's car pulled into a small parking lot in a trendy part of the city. Gavin parked a few spaces back, watching as Jason got out of the car and walked toward a building with a simple sign that read *Tranquil Flow Yoga Studio*. Gavin's brow furrowed.

Yoga?

Of course, he did yoga. It fit the picture of Jason perfectly—calm, composed, and always in control of himself. And now, here was another piece of the puzzle.

Gavin stepped out of his car, keeping a low profile as he followed Jason inside.

The studio was serene, filled with the soft scent of cedarwood and eucalyptus. Natural light streamed through large windows, casting a warm glow over the space. The walls were painted in soft earth tones, and lush plants were scattered throughout the room, creating a peaceful, almost otherworldly atmosphere. The front desk was clean and tranquil, with a small, delicate fountain trickling water nearby. A wall to the left showcased information about the various instructors, including their schedules and biographies.

Gavin's heart raced as he approached the wall, glancing over at the reception desk to ensure no one was watching. His eyes quickly scanned the neatly printed flyers until he found it—Jason Bringham, part-time yoga instructor. There was a photo of Jason in a relaxed yoga pose, looking as calm and centered as ever, his bio explaining his passion for teaching music and yoga as part of a balanced life. Below the bio, his class schedule was neatly listed: Tuesdays and Thursdays at the studio in the evening and a weekend morning session outdoors.

Gavin pulled out his phone and quickly snapped a picture of Jason's schedule, capturing all the details. His hands trembled slightly as he did it, the weight of his actions pressing down on him. But he had to know more. He needed more information—he needed to understand how deep Jason's connection to Eric ran and how long this betrayal had been happening.

Once he had the photo, Gavin turned on his heel and headed for the door, his heart still pounding. He didn't want to stay any longer than necessary. The air outside felt cooler and sharper as he stepped out of the studio and returned to his car. His mind was racing, trying to process everything he had learned. Jason wasn't just a music teacher—he was part of this whole other world that Gavin hadn't even known existed. How much of Eric's life had been wrapped up in Jason's?

As he got back into his car, Gavin stared down at the phone in his hand, the photo of Jason's yoga schedule glaring back at him like a piece of evidence in a crime. *This is it*, Gavin thought. *This is the thread I need to pull.*

He had no idea where this would lead, but one thing was certain—Jason Bringham was at the center of whatever had been happening between Eric and him. And Gavin wasn't going to stop until he uncovered the truth.

With a final glance at the yoga studio, Gavin started the car and drove away, the weight of his mission pressing heavily on his chest.

The hot water from the shower cascaded down Gavin's back, mingling with the tears he could no longer hold back. The heat from the water didn't soothe him; instead, it felt as though it only highlighted the cold emptiness plaguing his insides. His hands pressed against the cool tiles of the shower wall as he bowed his head, water running through his hair and over his face. The steady stream drowned out the muffled sobs that wracked his body, but it couldn't wash away either the pain or the betrayal that sat heavily on his chest.

His mind raced with the fresh discovery of Jason Bringham's other life. A music teacher and a yoga instructor, of all things—two faces to the same man who had been quietly, insidiously, slipping into his own life. Into Eric's life. How long had they been seeing each other? How long had Eric been lying to him, hiding this affair, all while playing the part of the perfect husband and father?

Gavin's sobs intensified, the weight of it all crashing down on him. The steam from the shower curled around him like a suffocating cloud, and he slid down to sit on the shower floor, pulling his knees to his chest. For a long time, he simply let the water fall, the tears blending with the steady stream, his chest rising and falling with the effort to breathe through the overwhelming sadness and rage.

He was drowning—drowning in a life that had slipped out of his control.

After what felt like an eternity, Gavin finally pulled himself up, his limbs heavy with exhaustion. He turned off the water, the sudden quiet in the bathroom almost deafening as the last few drops of water fell from the showerhead. He grabbed a towel and wrapped it around his waist, catching a glimpse of himself in the fogged mirror as he did. His face was pale, his eyes red and swollen from crying, and once he saw his reflection, he barely recognized himself.

He trudged out of the bathroom, wiping his face with the edge of the towel. As he dried off, changed, and walked out of the bedroom and into the kitchen, something caught his eye—the note on the fridge, a handwritten reminder that Ashton's birthday party was today. It was at the park.

Gavin just stood there, staring at the note, his heart constricting. *Ashton's birthday*. How had he let everything with Eric and Jason consume him so much that he had almost forgotten? Ashton's smile flashed in his mind—his bright, carefree smile, full of innocence and love. No matter what was happening between him and Eric, Ashton didn't deserve any of this. Ashton deserved a day filled with happiness, surrounded by his friends and family, without a shadow hanging over it.

Gavin took a deep breath and steeled himself. He could put all of this aside just for today. He had to for Ashton.

Gavin stood at the edge of the park, watching as the group of kids ran wildly around the playground, armed with Nerf guns and laughing at the top of their lungs. The bright afternoon sun warmed the air, the grass soft beneath his shoes as he surveyed the scene. Parents stood off to the side, chatting and keeping an eye on their kids, while Ashton and his friends darted between the trees and play structures, caught up in a game of tag.

Ashton's laughter rang through the air as he ducked behind a tree, evading a foam dart from one of his friends. Gavin couldn't help but smile, seeing his son so happy and carefree, easing the ache in his chest.

He pulled out his phone and snapped a few photos, capturing the scene—Ashton grinning ear to ear as he ran through the park, the sun casting a golden light over everything. Eric was standing nearby, watching Ashton with a smile that mirrored Gavin's. For a brief, bittersweet moment, Gavin felt that familiar warmth—this was his family, the one he had built and fought for. They looked perfect. But it was all a lie, wasn't it?

Gavin's smile faltered, his heart sinking as he glanced around the park again. It felt like something was missing—or rather, something was lurking just out of sight, which it actually was.

And then, he saw *him*.

Jason Bringham.

The music teacher—and now, the man who had inserted himself into Gavin's life in ways he could barely comprehend—was strolling up to the group. He wore casual clothes, jeans, and a simple shirt, but to Gavin, it felt like he was dressed for war. Jason walked with that same easy confidence that Gavin had seen before, that effortless charm that made everyone around him relax.

Including Eric.

Gavin's stomach twisted as he watched Jason approach Ashton and give him a high-five. Ashton beamed up at him, clearly happy to see his music teacher at his birthday party. Jason exchanged a few words with Ashton before glancing over at Eric, a subtle smile playing on his lips.

Gavin's blood boiled.

Eric had invited him here, to Ashton's birthday party. To their family event. Gavin's hands tightened into fists at his sides as he struggled to keep his composure. He wanted to march over there, to demand why Eric would bring this man into their lives so blatantly, so carelessly. But he couldn't make a scene—not here, not now. Not with Ashton and his friends running around, oblivious to the storm that was brewing just under the surface.

Gavin stood frozen, watching from a distance as Jason and Eric exchanged a few words, their interaction light and easy. Eric smiled—actually smiled—at something Jason said, and it made Gavin's stomach churn. How could Eric be so casual and carefree when Gavin's entire world was falling apart?

He looked away, unable to bear it any longer.

The rest of the party passed in a blur for Gavin. He tried his best to stay focused on Ashton, to engage with the other parents, and to help out where he could, but every time he glanced in Eric's direction, Jason was there. Jason laughing, Jason talking to Ashton, Jason standing just a little too close to Eric. And every time, Gavin's anger flared hotter, burning beneath his skin like a fire he couldn't extinguish.

By the time the party was winding down and the kids were beginning to pack up their Nerf guns, Gavin felt like he could barely breathe. He had managed to avoid Jason the entire time, keeping his distance and pretending like the man didn't exist, but the tension was unbearable.

As the parents gathered their kids and headed home, Gavin's eyes met Eric's from across the park. For that instance, he saw the man he had fallen in love with—the father of his child, the man who had once been his partner in everything. But now, there was a distance between them, a gulf that Gavin wasn't sure could ever be crossed again.

And it was all because of Jason.

As Gavin helped clean up the party, he knew one thing for certain: he couldn't avoid the confrontation any longer. He couldn't ignore what was happening. Eric had crossed a line by bringing Jason here into their family's world, and Gavin wasn't going to let it slide.

Ashton deserved better. *He* deserved better.

And it was time for Eric to know it.

The real estate office buzzed with the usual busy noise of phones ringing, keyboards clacking, and the quiet conversations of agents discussing properties with clients. The air smelled faintly of coffee and paper, and the glass windows let soft sunlight filter into the otherwise minimalist space. Amanda, the front office assistant, sat behind her desk, typing away at her computer, her polished nails clicking rhythmically against the keys. The peaceful atmosphere of the office was interrupted when the front door swung open, the bell above it chiming softly.

Wesley Daniels stormed inside.

His presence was a force that immediately shifted the energy in the room. Wesley was tall and broad-shouldered, his movements sharp with an underlying rage that seemed barely contained. His face was tight with discontent, his jaw clenched as his eyes scanned the office. The casual air of the real estate office seemed to mock him—its calmness in direct contrast to the storm brewing inside him. His fists were balled at his sides, and the set of his shoulders showed the strain of barely keeping himself in check.

Amanda looked up from her desk, her cheerful smile faltering as she saw Wesley. There was something about his rigid posture and the intensity in his eyes that set her on edge.

"Good afternoon," Amanda said, keeping her tone polite but guarded. "How can I help you?"

Wesley's gaze snapped to her, his eyes narrowing slightly. He took a deep breath before speaking, but it was clear that his patience was wearing thin.

"I'm here to see Gavin Hayes," Wesley said, his voice low but filled with a barely disguised edge. He wasn't in the mood for pleasantries, and it showed in the way his words came out clipped, each one carefully controlled.

Amanda blinked, her fingers pausing over the keyboard. "Gavin? Do you have an appointment with him?" she asked, her tone still professional but with an underlying wariness.

She could sense something was off, though she couldn't quite place it.

Wesley's jaw tightened even further, a muscle ticking at the side of his face. "No," he replied, his voice now laced with irritation. "But I need to speak with him. It's urgent."

Amanda's eyebrows knitted together, and she glanced at her computer screen, quickly pulling up Gavin's schedule. "I'm afraid Gavin has quite a few appointments today. He's in and out of the office, and there's a chance he might not be back at all today," she said cautiously, trying to keep her tone neutral.

Wesley's eyes flashed with frustration, and he let out a harsh breath, clearly not pleased with the response. He stepped closer to the desk, his imposing figure casting a shadow over Amanda. She resisted the urge to shrink back, keeping her professional demeanor intact.

"I'll wait for him," Wesley said firmly, his voice now dripping with impatience. "I'm not leaving until I see him."

Amanda shifted uncomfortably in her seat, her fingers drumming lightly against the desk. "Would you like to leave your name and number, Mr…?" She let the question hang, her voice trailing off in the hopes of getting a name.

Wesley's glare darkened. "No. I would *not* like to leave my name and number," he spat, his voice cold and dismissive. "I'll wait for as long as it takes. I have business with Gavin, and it's not something I plan on leaving a message about."

Amanda pursed her lips, trying to maintain her composure. The tension in the air was thick, and she could feel the simmering wrath radiating off Wesley. Something about his tone and the way he stood there, fists clenched, made her uneasy. "I understand," she replied carefully. "But I'm not sure how long Gavin will be—"

"I don't care how long it takes," Wesley interrupted, his voice rising slightly, though still controlled. He was on the edge, and it was clear he was barely holding himself together. "I'll be right here when he comes back."

Amanda swallowed, nodding slightly as she glanced at the empty chairs in the waiting area. "Alright, well… you're welcome to have a seat while you wait."

Wesley didn't respond, his lips pressing into a thin line as he walked stiffly to one of the chairs by the window. He sat down, his posture rigid, arms crossed over his chest, his foot tapping impatiently against the floor. His eyes darted toward the door every few seconds, as if willing Gavin to walk through it.

Amanda exhaled slowly, feeling the tension in the air growing heavier by the second. She knew something was wrong—this wasn't just a client wanting to speak with an agent. There was something more here, something darker. But she couldn't quite put her finger on it.

"I'll let Gavin know you're here as soon as I hear from him," she said softly, trying to maintain a calm presence. Wesley didn't acknowledge her, his focus entirely on the door, waiting, fuming.

Amanda cast one more cautious glance at Wesley before returning to her computer, her fingers hovering over the keys as she tried to go back to her work. But the oppressive energy of Wesley's presence lingered, making it impossible to shake the feeling that something was about to erupt.

Wesley's patience was thin, and the clock was ticking.

Chapter 12

Gavin sat in Dr. Jacobs' office, his arms crossed tightly over his chest, his leg bouncing nervously as he stared out the window. The office's usual calm and soothing atmosphere did nothing to ease the storm of emotions swirling inside him. His frustration boiled over, fueled by the rage that had been simmering ever since Ashton's birthday party at the park. Every time he closed his eyes, he could still see Jason Bringham high-fiving his son, laughing and smiling like he belonged there—like he had every right to be a part of their lives.

The mere thought of it made Gavin's skin crawl. *What was he even doing there? Why was Eric acting like everything was normal?*

Gavin's fingers dug into his arms as he tried to rein in his emotions, but the anger and confusion were too much. His voice came out sharp and bitter when he finally spoke. "They're all ganging up on me. He seriously came to my child's birthday party." He paused, his jaw clenched, his eyes darkening with the memory. "They're picking him over me."

Dr. Jacobs, sitting across from him with his usual calm expression, arched an eyebrow. "You really think your son is choosing him over you?" he asked, his voice measured and deliberate. He leaned back slightly in his chair, his hands resting on the armrests. "Does Ashton really even know him beyond school? Surely, he doesn't know his father is having an affair with him. You couldn't possibly think that."

Gavin's mouth opened to reply, but the words caught in his throat. He wanted to lash out, to say *yes*, and throw the blame at everyone else, but deep down, he knew Dr. Jacobs was right. Ashton was just a kid, caught up in the excitement of his birthday, oblivious to the adult drama playing out behind the scenes. But that didn't make it any easier to swallow the fact that Jason had shown up *uninvited*, and Eric had acted like it was perfectly normal.

"I don't know what to think anymore," Gavin finally muttered, his voice tight and strained. He rubbed his temples, feeling the tension build up in his head. "It's like everything's coming undone all at once. Eric, Jason, Ashton—everything's slipping through my fingers, and I can't seem to stop it."

Dr. Jacobs studied him, his eyes calm and calculating. "You feel out of control," he stated simply.

Gavin nodded, biting his lip as he tried to keep his emotions in check. "Yeah. I do. And seeing Jason there, at the park… it was like a slap in the face. Like he's already taking over, becoming part of our family, and I'm just… being pushed out."

Dr. Jacobs leaned forward slightly, his eyes locking onto Gavin's. "Do you believe that's really happening? Or is it that you fear it could happen?"

Gavin swallowed hard, his hands trembling slightly as they rested in his lap. "I don't know," he whispered. "I just—" He paused, searching for the right words, but they seemed to evade him. His thoughts were jumbled, like pieces of a puzzle that didn't fit together. He looked away, his gaze falling back to the window.

The silence between them stretched like a taut wire, the tension palpable in the room. Gavin continued staring out the window, trying to ground himself, but the memories bubbling up in his mind were too powerful, too vivid. He could feel Dr. Jacobs' eyes on him, waiting for him to continue, waiting for the truth to unravel. Gavin clenched his fists by his sides, his breath coming in short, sharp bursts.

Dr. Jacobs finally broke the silence. "I do want to talk more about your past," he said quietly, his voice calm but insistent. "When your parents weren't there for you."

Gavin huffed, his eyes still fixed on the world outside the window, though he wasn't really seeing it. "That's not even the half of it."

He turned then, pacing the length of the room as if the motion would somehow release the torrent of emotions building inside him. His hands ran through his hair, tugging at the strands in vexation.

"I already mentioned that when I was a kid, my mom was in and out of mental facilities," Gavin began, his voice low and bitter. "And while she was locked up, my dad… well, he didn't exactly cope in the healthiest ways." He laughed darkly, though there was no humor in it. "He'd bring women over. And men, too. Seedy people. I don't even know where he found them, but there they were, night after night, doing God knows what."

Gavin stopped pacing, standing still in the center of the room, his face contorted with outrage and pain. "I was just a kid. I didn't understand half of what was happening, but I knew it wasn't right. The worst part? Some of those men… they touched me. They'd come into my room when my dad was passed out cold, drunk or drugged off his ass."

Dr. Jacobs' eyes darkened, and his posture shifted slightly as if bracing himself for what Gavin would say next. Gavin's voice wavered as he spoke, the words slipping out like poison.

"I told my dad what they did. I told him everything." His voice cracked, and he swallowed hard, trying to keep the tears at bay. "And you know what he said? He told me to shut up. That I was lying. Said I was making it up for attention. Can you believe that?"

Dr. Jacobs' expression tightened, but he remained silent, giving Gavin the space to continue.

"But I did learn something about myself early on in those days," Gavin said, his voice dropping to almost a whisper. "I could capture the attention of men older than me. Charm them. It's what allowed me to survive when my dad left, and

I was all alone." He looked down at his hands as if seeing them for the first time. "When I was living on the streets, I met men—rich, older men—and they paid for my... *services*. It was the only way I could survive."

Gavin's voice grew hollow as he continued. "I did it for years. It's how I paid for community college. I bought nice clothes, made myself look the part. And then I aimed higher, getting the attention of even wealthier men. Men who could afford to pay more. It's what I had to do."

The weight of the confession settled over the room like a dark cloud. Gavin stood there, exposed, vulnerable in a way he hadn't been in years. He had never told anyone this—not even Eric.

Dr. Jacobs took a deep breath, his voice filled with quiet compassion. "That's... awful, Gavin. All of it. Hard to believe, even."

Gavin met his therapist's stare; his eyes hardened with the weight of his past. "Well, believe it."

Dr. Jacobs held Gavin's gaze, his face thoughtful, trying to process everything Gavin had just revealed. "Does Eric know any of this?" he asked gently.

Gavin shook his head, his jaw tightening. "No. He has no idea. If he had known, he would never have married me. He's perfect. He comes from this perfect family. No skeletons in the closet. Nothing messy like this."

Dr. Jacobs leaned forward slightly, his expression serious. "You don't know that, Gavin. You can't assume Eric would reject you just because of your past. You've kept this part of yourself hidden, but that doesn't mean it defines you."

Gavin looked away, his throat tight with emotion. "Eric's not like that. He wouldn't be able to handle it. He's all about appearances, about being proper. A past like mine? It wouldn't play well for him."

He felt the tears welling up again but forced them back down, unwilling to let himself break. He stood up abruptly, walking over to the window, needing to escape the suffocating weight of the conversation. He pressed his hands against the glass, staring out at the street below but seeing nothing.

"I think I just realized something," Gavin said, his voice barely audible. "Maybe that's why Colton appeals to me so much. I'm meant to be with guys like him. Guys who don't expect anything more than sex. No strings, no commitment. That's all I'm good for."

Dr. Jacobs' voice was soft, but insistent. "But you told me you think Colton loves you, right? Do you honestly believe that, Gavin?"

Gavin turned around, his face filled with confusion and pain. "I do. I mean, I think he does. But I'm not sure Eric loves me anymore." He hesitated, his voice trembling. "I don't want to lose everything again. I won't let my past ruin my life. You don't think it's too late, do you?"

Dr. Jacobs stood up slowly, his gaze steady and filled with empathy. "No, Gavin," he said softly. "It's not too late. You're not your past. And if Eric truly loves you, he'll stand by you, no matter what."

Gavin let out a shaky breath, his chest tightening with both relief and uncertainty. He wanted to believe Dr. Jacobs. He wanted to believe that it wasn't too late, that he hadn't already lost everything he cared about. But the shadow of his past still loomed large, and it was hard to see the light through all the darkness.

For now, though, he would hold on to the hope that maybe, just maybe, it wasn't too late after all.

Chapter 13

The early morning sunlight filtered through the trees, casting long, golden rays over the trail that wound through the mountainside. The crisp air carried the scent of pine and damp earth, mingling with the soft murmur of the breeze rustling the leaves. The yoga class had been set up on a flat, open stretch of the trail, surrounded by towering pines and the sounds of nature. The faint chirping of birds and the distant trickle of a stream added a sense of serenity to the space, a perfect backdrop for meditation and stretching.

Jason Bringham, dressed in loose, comfortable yoga attire, stood at the front of the group of thirty participants, his voice calm and soothing as he guided them through the final stretch. His movements were fluid and effortless, as he demonstrated the poses with quiet authority.

Gavin, positioned in the back of the group, mirrored Jason's movements, but his mind was elsewhere. He hadn't come for the peaceful yoga practice—he had come for Jason.

As the final pose came to an end, Jason instructed the group to slowly rise and thank their bodies for the practice. Everyone soon rolled up their mats and began to disperse, chatting quietly as they made their way back down the trail toward the parking lot. Gavin remained behind, watching Jason as he carefully packed up his things.

The mountain air was cool, but Gavin felt the heat rising within him. His chest tightened with nervous energy and pent-up anger as he approached Jason. The clearing was empty now, the other participants gone, leaving only the two of them standing among the towering trees.

Jason looked up from his mat, noticing Gavin lingering. He raised an eyebrow, a friendly smile playing on his lips.

"Do I know you?" he asked, his voice casual but curious.

Gavin felt his heart race. He had rehearsed what he wanted to say in his head over and over, but now that he was standing here, facing Jason, the words felt tangled in his throat.

"I don't think we've been introduced," Gavin replied, his voice steady despite his inner turmoil.

Jason's expression brightened with recognition. "Oh yes! I've seen you at a few of the school recitals," he said, rolling up his mat and tucking it under his arm. "What grade is your child in?"

"Third grade," Gavin answered, his eyes locked on Jason's, searching for any sign of guilt or indication that he knew who Gavin really was.

Jason laughed lightly, his voice easy. "Oh! That's ironic. Mine is, too."

The two men began walking together down the mountain trail, the sound of their footsteps crunching softly against the dirt and gravel. The path wound its way through the trees, offering breathtaking views of the valley below, but Gavin barely noticed the beauty around him. His mind was fixated on one thing: confronting the man who had stolen his husband.

After a few moments of silence, Gavin spoke again, his voice carrying a weight that made Jason glance over at him with a slight frown. "I'll be honest," Gavin began, his tone low, "I actually didn't come here for yoga today. I came here looking for you."

Jason stopped walking for a second, turning to Gavin with a puzzled expression. "Me?" he asked, his tone light but with a hint of confusion. He chuckled awkwardly, as if trying to make light of the situation. "What do you mean?"

Gavin continued walking, his footsteps slower and more deliberate. "I know what you've been doing with my husband."

The casual air between them evaporated instantly. Jason's face shifted, his friendly demeanor replaced with bewilderment. "Your husband?" Jason said, his brow furrowed. "What are you talking about?"

Gavin felt the rage he had been holding back for so long surge to the surface. He stopped walking, turning to face Jason with a look of cold fury. "Don't play games with me. I know what you've been doing with him."

Jason took a step back, clearly caught off guard by the sudden shift in Gavin's tone. "What the hell are you talking about?" he demanded, his voice rising in confusion and frustration. "Are you crazy? I don't know anything about you or your husband."

The rage that had been simmering inside Gavin boiled over. He could feel his pulse pounding in his ears, his vision narrowing as the accusation left his lips, sharper and more vicious than before. "Liar!" Gavin shouted, his voice echoing through the trees. "I saw you with him. I saw everything!"

Jason's eyes widened, his face pale with shock. "I don't know what you think you saw, but you're wrong," he insisted, his voice shaky now, panic creeping into his words. "I don't even know who your husband is. You're fucking crazy!"

But Gavin didn't believe him. The image of Jason and Eric together, laughing and sharing secret glances, burned in his mind, fueling his anger. Without thinking, without considering the consequences, Gavin acted.

Before he could stop himself, Gavin shoved Jason hard. Jason stumbled backward, his foot slipping on the loose gravel of the trail. His arms flailed as he tried to catch his balance, but it was too late. He toppled over the edge of the trail, disappearing down the steep hillside.

The sound of Jason's body crashing through the underbrush was sickening. Gavin stood frozen in place, his breath caught in his throat as he watched Jason's body tumble down the rocky slope. Time seemed to slow as Jason's head struck a large boulder with a sickening thud. His body movement limp, crumpling against the rocks, blood pooling around his head.

For a moment, there was only silence. The sound of the wind through the trees and the distant calls of birds faded into the background as Gavin stared in stunned disbelief at what he had just done.

His heart pounded in his chest, and his breath came in short, ragged gasps. He hadn't meant for it to go this far. He hadn't meant to push him. But now Jason lay motionless at the bottom of the slope, his body twisted at an unnatural angle, blood seeping into the earth.

Panic seized Gavin as reality crashed over him. *What have I done?* His mind raced, wild and frantic. He couldn't stay here. He couldn't be found. His pulse quickened, and without another thought, Gavin turned and ran.

His feet pounded against the trail, his breath coming in sharp gasps as he sprinted away from the scene. The trees blurred past him, the mountain air burning in his lungs as he pushed himself to move faster. *Don't stop. Don't look back.*

His thoughts were a jumble of fear and regret, each one crashing into the next. *What if someone saw us? What if they find him?* His mind raced with worst-case scenarios, but he couldn't stop. He had to get out of there. He had to escape before it was too late.

As he ran, the image of Jason's lifeless body burned in his mind, a constant, horrific reminder of what he had done. However, Gavin could not lie to himself. A sense of relief did wash over him now that he realized Jason was out of the picture. He could already sense that his relationship with Eric would surely be better now.

Chapter 14

The warm, late afternoon sunlight filtered through the large windows of Dr. Jacobs' office, casting a soft glow over the room. The familiar, earthy scent of lavender filled the air, and the usual serene atmosphere seemed to have an extra layer of calmness today. Gavin sat comfortably in the chair across from Dr. Jacobs, a small, contented smile playing on his lips as he sipped from his water bottle. His body language was relaxed, his movements smooth and easy, a stark contrast to the tense, brooding figure he had been in recent weeks.

Dr. Jacobs observed him carefully, noting the change in demeanor. Gavin was almost perky today; his usual intensity softened as though a great weight had been lifted from his shoulders.

"You seem rather chipper," Dr. Jacobs remarked, folding his hands in his lap as he leaned back in his chair. His eyes narrowed slightly, studying Gavin's face. "What's going on?"

Gavin let out a soft chuckle, his fingers idly tapping on the armrest of his chair. "Things are getting better," he replied, his voice light, almost carefree. "Everything's falling into place. You know how it is—one minute, life feels like it's crumbling, and the next, everything just clicks."

Dr. Jacobs raised an eyebrow, intrigued by the sudden shift in Gavin's attitude. "What about the other guy?" he asked, his tone probing but gentle. "The music teacher."

Gavin waved his hand dismissively, as though brushing away an insignificant thought. "Gone. It's over between Eric and him."

Dr. Jacobs paused, carefully choosing his next words. "Are you sure?" he asked, his voice calm but tinged with skepticism.

"Positive," Gavin said, nodding confidently. His smile widened, a satisfied gleam in his eyes. "Eric and I talked it out. Everything's been handled. Jason's not an issue anymore."

"You must be really relieved," Dr. Jacobs said, watching Gavin closely for any signs of hesitation or lingering doubt.

Gavin's expression softened, and for a moment, a hint of vulnerability crossed his face. "Relieved isn't even the word," he said, his voice lowering slightly. "I'm grateful… just… so grateful. I've got my life back. My family back."

Dr. Jacobs gave a slight nod, leaning forward slightly. "And what about Colton?" he asked, his eyes never leaving Gavin's.

The smile on Gavin's face didn't falter, but his eyes flickered with something unreadable. "Done," he said simply. "I don't need him anymore. My life with Eric is working now."

Dr. Jacobs tilted his head, a small crease forming between his brows. "That easy, huh?"

Gavin shrugged, his posture still relaxed. "That easy," he repeated, his voice firm.

Dr. Jacobs pressed on. "What if Colton calls you again? What if he says he wants you back?"

Gavin sighed, a faint smile playing on his lips as if the answer didn't bother him in the slightest. "He already has called," Gavin admitted, leaning back in his chair. "He told me how much he misses me. It was… sweet. Romantic. He wanted to take me back to his art gallery where we first met." He laughed softly, the memory almost amusing to him now.

Dr. Jacobs' expression tightened, a flash of confusion crossing his face. He remained silent, then spoke carefully, his tone measured. "Ummm, wait a minute," he said, his voice tinged with mild skepticism. "I don't remember you telling me that. No. I thought you said you met Colton at a local bar or nightclub? He sent you a drink, if I recall correctly."

Gavin blinked, his smile fading just slightly. He shook his head. "Well, yeah," he replied, his tone casual but slightly defensive. "We went to the bar after that night at the art gallery. We had drinks later, but the gallery is where we first met."

Dr. Jacobs leaned back in his chair, his fingers steepled under his chin as he carefully studied Gavin. "That sounds lovely," he said, his voice neutral, but there was an undercurrent of doubt that Gavin seemed to miss.

A long silence followed, the room filled with the ticking of the clock on the wall. Dr. Jacobs was deep in thought, piecing together the discrepancy in Gavin's story. Once he reflected, he spoke again, his voice gentle but pointed. "Hmmm. I do have to say, Gavin, I doubt that's something I would forget. Yes, I'm certain you said you first laid eyes on Colton at the bar. Not the art gallery."

Gavin waved his hand dismissively, as if the conversation was tedious. "No. We met at the art gallery," he said, his tone growing slightly irritated. "That first night was like magic." He paused, the irritation in his voice giving way to nostalgia. "Anyway, back to reality. Back to my life."

Dr. Jacobs' eyes lingered on Gavin, allowing the small, creeping doubt to grow stronger in his mind. But for now, he said nothing. Instead, he simply nodded, allowing the conversation to move on.

But things were not adding up. He couldn't shake the feeling that Gavin's story wasn't completely accurate. Dr. Jacobs studied Gavin closely. Something felt off, though he couldn't immediately pinpoint what it was. Gavin had been calm, even cheerful, today, but there was a distance in his responses, a gloss over the usual emotion that worried Dr. Jacobs.

"I'm glad you see things so clearly," Dr. Jacobs said, his voice measured and careful. He watched for Gavin's reaction, searching for cracks in the façade.

Gavin grinned, the confidence radiating off of him like

heat from the pavement. "I always know when it's time to walk away," he replied, his tone light, as though this were something simple—obvious.

Dr. Jacobs frowned slightly, leaning forward in his chair. "How do you know that?" he asked, his voice gentle but probing.

Gavin shrugged as if the answer was the most natural thing in the world. "It's just a thing," he began, his voice easy and smooth. "I've experienced it most of my life, even before I met Eric. Guys have always had a thing for me. Then, after a while, they get… well, *crazy*. *Obsessive*. And when I can't make them realize what we actually are—or aren't—I have to go. I shut it down before things get too out of hand."

Dr. Jacobs listened, nodding slowly, but his mind churned. Gavin's tone was too casual, too detached from the gravity of what he was describing. Something about it didn't sit right. He pressed on carefully. "That must be very difficult," Dr. Jacobs said, his voice calm and understanding.

Gavin sighed, almost dramatically, as if the weight of his experiences was something he had long grown used to. "It is," he said, his tone softening, though his eyes remained sharp. "Sometimes it's frightening. There were a few times when it got so bad that I had to disappear completely. Leave without a trace so they couldn't find me." He paused, glancing out the window before continuing. "But that was long ago, before Eric. My life is different now. It's perfect."

Dr. Jacobs raised an eyebrow, still feeling the disconnect between Gavin's words and demeanor. "That must have been a very unsettling way to live," he said, trying to draw out more from Gavin and get him to acknowledge the emotional toll that such a life would have taken.

Gavin waved it off with a casual flick of his hand. "Like I said, it's in the past. I don't need to worry about that anymore. My life with Eric is solid. Colton's out of the picture. Jason's out of the picture. I'm good."

Gavin paused, then added, "Listen, I appreciate everything you've done for me, but I won't be coming back." His smile widened, and he sat up a little straighter in his chair. "Now that my life is straightening out, I just don't see the point."

Dr. Jacobs' brow furrowed, and a sense of dread settled in his gut. "Gavin, it's never this simple," he said carefully, his eyes fixed on Gavin's face, trying to gauge his reaction.

Gavin's smile faltered slightly, but his tone remained light, though there was an edge of annoyance creeping in. "Um, I'm sorry, but in my case, it is." He crossed his arms seeming offended, his posture stiffening ever so slightly.

Dr. Jacobs pressed on, feeling the need to push further. "No. I don't think so," he said, his tone firm but still calm. "There are things that you've told me that have me very concerned. The way you deal with your relationships, for example. Your recollections... they've differed from one session to the next. You've told me different versions of the same events on multiple occasions."

Gavin's eyes narrowed, and his smile was completely gone now. His voice grew defensive. "No. No. I maybe embellished or carried on a little, maybe exaggerated," he said, waving his hand dismissively. "But I'm fine. I'm really fine."

Dr. Jacobs' concern deepened. "Gavin, I'm not comfortable with—"

But Gavin cut him off, standing up abruptly, his movements sharp and deliberate. "No, really, I am," he insisted, brushing off Dr. Jacobs' words as though they meant nothing. He turned, already heading for the door, his shoulders set in a way that suggested he had made up his mind.

Dr. Jacobs felt a sense of defeat settle over him. He had been trying to reach Gavin to make him see that there were deeper issues at play, but it seemed like Gavin had already decided he was done.

Still, Dr. Jacobs couldn't just let him walk away without trying one more time. "Well," he said softly, his voice tinged with concern. "At least keep in touch so I know how you're doing."

Gavin stopped at the door, his hand on the knob. He glanced over his shoulder, his expression unreadable. "That won't be necessary," he said, his voice cool, detached. Without another word, he opened the door and walked out, the sound of it clicking shut behind him echoing in the now-empty room.

Dr. Jacobs sat back in his chair, staring at the closed door. His mind whirled with thoughts, but one thing stood out clearly: something was deeply wrong, and Gavin wasn't willing—or able—to see it.

Chapter 15

The following day, Gavin strolled into the office, his gait confident and his head held high. The office was buzzing with the usual activity—agents on the phone with clients, the loud racket of printers working overtime, and the occasional burst of laughter from a colleague's cubicle. Sunlight streamed through the floor-to-ceiling windows, casting long shadows across the glossy floors, and the faint scent of coffee lingered in the air. Everything seemed... *normal*.

Gavin relished the sense of control he felt. The anxiety and tension that had plagued him in recent weeks had lifted, replaced by a smooth sense of calm. After all, he had dealt with everything, hadn't he? Colton was out of the picture. Eric's wandering eye had been handled. And Jason? Well, that was a closed chapter, *literally*.

But just as Gavin reached his office door, his hand on the knob, a voice called out behind him.

"Mr. Hayes?"

He turned slowly, the smile still on his lips but faltering slightly when he saw a man standing in the middle of the open office area. The man was out of place amidst the polished real estate agents in their designer suits, shoes, and heels. He was in his mid-fifties, his face hard and chiseled, with a thick salt-and-pepper mustache and piercing blue eyes that seemed to see straight through you. He wore a tan trench coat over his button-down shirt, and a badge clipped to his belt glinted in the light.

The pit of Gavin's stomach dropped, but he maintained his composure, letting his eyebrows rise in what he hoped was a casual gesture of surprise. "Yes, I'm Gavin Hayes. Can I help you?"

The man stepped forward, his face unreadable. "Detective Miller," he said, holding out his hand.

Gavin shook it, feeling the firmness in the detective's grip. "A detective? What can I do for you?" he asked, injecting a note of curiosity into his voice while his heart beat just a little faster.

Detective Miller glanced around the busy office. "Could we speak in private?"

"Of course," Gavin said, gesturing toward his office door. "Come in."

He opened the door and ushered the detective inside. Gavin moved behind his desk, the familiar surroundings calming him somewhat as he slid into his chair. Detective Miller remained standing, surveying the room, before finally sitting down across from Gavin, the leather of the chair creaking softly under his weight.

"I'm here to ask a few questions," Detective Miller began, his voice steady and professional. "It's regarding Jason Bringham."

Gavin's pulse quickened, but he kept his expression neutral, his eyebrows furrowing slightly as though hearing the name for the first time in a while. "Jason Bringham?" he repeated, acting as if he needed a second to place the name. "Wait… the yoga instructor?"

Miller's gaze sharpened, his eyes studying Gavin's reaction. "Yes, the yoga instructor. I understand you attended one of his classes recently?"

Gavin leaned back in his chair, feigning casual surprise. "Yes, I took a recent yoga class with him," he said, his voice laced with a mix of curiosity and confusion. "Is something wrong? Why are you asking about him?"

Detective Miller shifted slightly in his seat, his eyes never leaving Gavin's. "Jason Bringham is dead."

The words hit the room like a stone dropped into still water. Gavin felt his stomach lurch, but outwardly, he played the part, his eyes widening in shock. "Oh my god," he whispered, his hand coming up to his mouth in disbelief. "I had no idea. That's... that's awful."

Miller nodded slowly, watching Gavin's reaction closely. "Yes, it is. We're still gathering information, but I'm speaking to everyone who was at that class, trying to understand what happened in the hours leading up to his death that day. He was found off the mountain trail supposedly having fallen down the slope. Hit his head on a nearby boulder. Bled to death."

Gavin leaned forward, his face pale, eyes wide. "Oh my God! How awful! Well, I don't know what I can tell you," he said, his voice soft and hesitant. "I didn't really pay much attention to anything that day, really. Nothing seemed out of the ordinary."

Miller's gaze was unwavering. "One of the yoga participants recalls seeing someone matching your description as one of the last people present after the class."

Gavin blinked, leaning back in his chair as though trying to recall. "I guess it's possible," he said slowly, shrugging as if the memory was faint. "I don't really remember. I was in my own head that day."

He paused, then added, "I last saw him packing up his mat. That's about it."

Miller's eyes narrowed slightly, but his voice remained calm. "Was anyone else with him at the time?"

Gavin hesitated, then shook his head. "Honestly, I don't even remember," he said, his voice growing more distant. "I had a lot on my mind that day. I'm actually embarrassed to tell you what I was really thinking about when something so... so horrific then happened."

The detective leaned forward slightly, his voice coaxing. "Please, indulge me. I hear it all."

Gavin sighed, his hand coming up to his forehead as if overwhelmed by the memory. "Well, the holidays are coming up, and I was thinking about dinners, hosting family, my son's extracurricular activities—he's into baseball now, and his trumpet lessons, you know." He chuckled softly, the sound almost self-deprecating. "I guess that's why I was at yoga in the first place. Just trying to clear my mind. But I wasn't paying much attention to anyone else after I left. It seemed... insignificant at the time."

Detective Miller nodded slowly, his face unreadable. "I see. Well, thank you for your time, Mr. Hayes." He reached into his coat and pulled out a small card, sliding it across the desk toward Gavin. "Here's my number. If anything else comes to mind, no matter how small, give me a call."

Gavin picked up the card, glancing at it before looking back up at the detective with a polite smile. "Of course. Thank you, detective. I'll let you know if I think of anything."

Detective Miller stood, his eyes still trained on Gavin as though trying to read something deeper beneath the surface. "I'll be in touch," he said, nodding once before turning to leave.

As the door clicked shut behind him, Gavin let out a slow breath, the tension he had been holding onto releasing slightly. He stared down at the detective's card, the weight of the encounter sinking in. His mind raced, the carefully crafted façade he had maintained during the conversation starting to crack under the pressure.

But then he shook his head, pushing the thoughts away. He had handled it. He always did. Everything would be fine.

Chapter 16

Gavin stood in the sunlit living room of the Fontina Beach House, his refined demeanor matching the gorgeous lines of the opulent yet cozy home he was showing. The place was immaculate, with floor-to-ceiling windows offering a breathtaking view of the ocean, and the fresh scent of sea salt wafted in from the breeze outside. The interior had a crisp, coastal design—whitewashed walls, light oak floors, and a stunning open-concept kitchen with clean marble countertops. The sparkling blue of the sea was the perfect backdrop, and Gavin could feel the energy in the room shift as his client, a man in his mid-forties with a sharp suit and an even sharper mind, took in the luxurious surroundings.

"This place is exactly what I've been looking for," the client said, his tone filled with satisfaction as he walked over to the large windows and gazed out at the ocean. "The location, the design, everything. I need to make this happen, and I need it to happen fast."

Gavin smiled, his sharp instincts already kicking in. This was the time to close. "It's an exceptional property," he replied smoothly, his voice confident but measured. "And it's rare to find something like this at Fontina Beach. The sellers have had a few strong offers, but I think if we move quickly, this can be yours without a hitch."

The client turned, his expression decisive. "I want to expedite escrow. We need to close fast—fifteen days, if possible. No contingencies. No inspections. I'm ready to move on this, all cash, fifty-thousand above asking price."

Gavin's mind was already running through the logistics. The beach house was a hot property, and with this being an all-cash offer and above asking price, there was a very good chance they could push the deal through quickly. But he knew he had to get the sellers on board.

"Fifteen days? No problem. I think we should be able to make that work without the inspections. Give me a minute," Gavin requested, pulling out his phone to dial Spencer, who had the direct line to the sellers. He spoke to his client once more. "Let me confirm with the sellers and their agent. They're motivated, but we need to make sure they're on board with the timing."

He stepped aside, feeling the sun warm his skin as he stood by the patio doors that led out to the beachfront deck.

The phone rang twice before Spencer picked up.

"Spencer, it's Gavin. I'm at the Fontina Beach House," Gavin said briskly. "The client is ready to move forward, but he wants to expedite escrow—fifteen days. No contingencies or inspections. It's an all-cash sale and fifty-thousand dollars above the asking price; loans aren't an issue."

Spencer was quiet for a second while processing the request. Gavin could hear him typing something on his end, likely texting the sellers to get their agreement. "Fifteen days is tight, but if it's cash with no inspections, we might be able to swing it," Spencer replied. "Let me text them right now."

Gavin paced slightly, his eyes scanning the property as he waited. The client was still admiring the house, running his hand along the marble countertop in the kitchen and peering into the spacious dining area. Gavin's pulse quickened as he thought about sealing the deal. This wasn't just a sale—this was the kind of transaction that solidified reputations in the real estate business.

A second later, Spencer's voice crackled back over the phone. "Okay, they're in. The sellers will agree to a fifteen-day escrow, which is no problem. It's a deal."

Gavin smiled, his heart racing. "Perfect," he said, keeping his voice composed, but the excitement was unmistakable. "Thanks, Spencer. I'll move forward on my end."

THE TROMPE L'OEIL EFFECT

"Perfect. You're amazing, as always," Spencer complimented.

Gavin ended the call and turned back to his client, who was now standing in the middle of the living room, clearly eager to hear the verdict.

"Good news," Gavin announced, his smile broad. "The sellers are on board with a fifteen-day escrow. All we need is your signature on a few documents, which I'll get you right away when I get back to my office, and this place is yours."

The client grinned, his eyes lighting up with satisfaction. "That's exactly what I wanted to hear. Let's get it done."

They shook hands, sealing the deal, and Gavin could already envision the paperwork coming together. His mind raced with the final steps—getting the contracts signed, ensuring everything moved smoothly with the title company—but for now, he allowed himself a respite to savor the victory. The Fontina Beach House was as good as sold, and this would be another feather in his cap.

As they made their way to the door, Gavin could feel the rush of adrenaline—the high of the deal. He'd done it again.

The soft clinking of glasses and the low volume of quiet conversation filled the air as Gavin walked into an upscale restaurant. It was an elegant place, with dark wood paneling, dimly lit by candlelight, and large windows that looked out over the city skyline. The ambiance was intimate yet refined, with soft jazz playing in the background and sleek leather chairs arranged around tables draped in white linen. The rich aroma of freshly cooked meals and fine wine filled the space, creating an inviting warmth. It was the kind of restaurant designed for special occasions—perfect for Gavin's current state of mind.

As Gavin was led to a table by the hostess, he felt a wave of satisfaction from the day's success. The sale of the Fontina Beach House had gone off without a hitch, and now, he was planning the next big move with the hefty commission check he'd be receiving from the sale: a private getaway with Eric, something to reconnect and bask in after the recent whirlwind of their lives. Gavin had selected this place to meet with his travel agent, knowing the atmosphere would set the tone for the romantic trip he envisioned.

The table was set by a window, the city twinkling just outside as Gavin sat down, drumming his fingers lightly on the menu before the travel agent arrived. A glass of sparkling water was already waiting for him, beads of condensation running down the side as he took a sip, glancing around the restaurant. The place exuded luxury, from the high vaulted ceilings to the artfully arranged floral centerpieces on each table. It reminded Gavin of the kind of life he and Eric had worked so hard to build—a life filled with elegance and refinement.

Soon after Gavin arrived, the travel agent, a woman named Melanie with neatly styled hair and a poised demeanor, approached the table. She wore a tailored blazer and had a tablet tucked under her arm, exuding efficiency and professionalism. "Gavin, so lovely to see you again," she greeted warmly as she took her seat.

"Thanks for meeting me on such short notice," Gavin replied, offering her a charming smile. He was eager, almost restless, to set the wheels in motion for this trip.

"Of course," Melanie said as she settled in, placing her tablet on the table and opening it up to a travel itinerary template. "So, what can I do for you? I understand you're looking to plan a special getaway."

Gavin leaned forward slightly, his fingers tapping thoughtfully on the edge of the table. "Yes, I want to plan something for Eric. Something that'll sweep him off his feet," he said, his tone filled with excitement. "I've been thinking... the Maldives. Definitely a beach destination, somewhere private and pampering. A place where we can completely escape."

Melanie nodded as she made a few quick notes on her tablet. "The Maldives are a fantastic choice for that. Private villas, crystal-clear waters, lots of seclusion. Are you thinking something luxurious? Overwater bungalow, perhaps?"

"Exactly," Gavin said, his smile widening. "I want this to be a surprise. No distractions, no one else. Just the two of us."

Melanie glanced up from her tablet, her expression thoughtful. "That sounds perfect. And I assume you'll want something all-inclusive? Spa treatments, private dinners, maybe even some excursions like snorkeling or a private yacht cruise?"

"Absolutely," Gavin replied, leaning back in his chair as he let the idea settle in his mind. "Completely indulgent. This has to be something we both remember for a long time."

A sudden thought crossed his mind, and he hesitated before speaking. "Actually," Gavin began, his brow furrowing slightly, "I was thinking Ashton might enjoy something like this, too. He loves the water, and I know he'd get a kick out of a place like that. Should I bring him?"

Melanie looked up with a polite smile, ready to adjust the plan. "We can certainly arrange something for the whole family if you'd like."

Gavin paused, his eyes narrowing as he considered it. But then, as the idea of bringing Ashton along sunk in, he realized this trip needed to be about him and Eric. "No," he said firmly, shaking his head. "This needs to be just us two. Ashton's been a part of everything lately, and we love him, but this is something we need for ourselves."

Melanie nodded again, understanding. "A romantic week for two, then. I'll focus on the details—private dinners on the beach, sunset boat cruises, spa days. Everything will be personalized to make it a perfect experience for you and Eric."

"Exactly what we need," Gavin said, his voice softening as he envisioned the two of them walking along the white sandy beaches of the Maldives, the waves gently lapping at their feet, their relationship rekindling under the warmth of the tropical sun. "This is just what we need right now," Gavin repeated, picturing the spectacular getaway. "Eric will be blown away by this surprise trip."

Melanie smiled, typing away on her tablet. "I'll get everything arranged. You won't have to lift a finger once you're there."

"Perfect," Gavin said, his voice filled with satisfaction. He took another sip of his water, feeling a sense of contentment wash over him. For the first time in a while, things were falling into place. He had Eric, their life together, and now, the perfect getaway to solidify it all.

Melanie finished entering the details and looked up, her professional tone returning. "I'll send over the itinerary later this week. You'll have all the options laid out, and we can finalize everything from there."

Gavin nodded, standing up and extending his hand. "Thank you, Melanie. I appreciate you helping me pull this together."

"It's my pleasure, Gavin," she said with a smile as they shook hands. "You're going to love it. And I'm sure Eric will, too."

As Gavin left the restaurant, the cool evening breeze swept over him, but inside, he felt nothing but warmth. He could already picture the two of them—away from everything, away from the complications of their everyday lives. It was exactly what they needed.

For the first time in a long time, Gavin felt hopeful.

Dr. Jacobs sat alone in his office, the familiar ticking of the wall clock punctuating the silence around him. The room, as always, was bathed in the soft glow of the late afternoon sun filtering through the blinds, casting long, golden stripes across the plush beige carpeting. The consistent scent of lavender from the diffuser mingled with the rich, earthy tones of the wooden bookshelves lining the walls, creating an air of serenity. But today, despite the tranquility of his surroundings, Dr. Jacobs felt an unsettling heaviness in the pit of his stomach.

He sat behind his desk, a small digital recorder lying in front of him, its red light blinking steadily once he pressed the record button. His fingers, usually steady and sure, trembled slightly as he adjusted the recorder closer.

"Patient presents himself as a normal gay uptown guy," Dr. Jacobs began, his voice steady but with an underlying tension. He glanced out the window as though the words he needed were hanging somewhere outside. "Patient describes being in a boring marriage, yet also an exciting affair."

His eyes drifted across the room, landing on the worn leather chair where Gavin had sat just the day before, exuding confidence and detachment in equal measure. It was the same chair where so many patients had shared their lives, their secrets, and their fears—but with Gavin, something was different.

Dr. Jacobs ran a hand through his graying hair, his fingers lingering at the nape of his neck as he continued speaking into the recorder. "But lately, his behavior has been becoming more and more... *alarming*. Disconnected, rather. While he may not show the usual signs of depression, his mood is often neutral and lacking in emotion." His voice wavered slightly on the last word, the tone of a man who had seen enough to know when something was deeply wrong.

He paused, leaning back in his chair as the sound of a car horn honked faintly from the street below. It was a rare disturbance in this usually quiet part of town, and he wondered if the honk felt like a jarring note in an otherwise composed melody—much like Gavin's sessions had become.

"Yet his descriptions of Colton," Dr. Jacobs continued, a crease forming between his brows. "The subject of his affair, seem embellished and glorified. There's a stark contrast between how he describes his relationship with Eric and this... *affair*. With Colton, there's this fantastical quality—everything about their interactions is heightened, romanticized, almost cinematic. It's as though he's constructing a narrative."

Dr. Jacobs' gaze shifted to his notepad, where he had jotted down various fragmented versions of how Gavin had first met Colton. It seemed that the details shifted slightly with each session. First, they met at a bar. Then, it was an art gallery. The timeline of their affair seemed to bend and warp, and the inconsistencies gnawed at Dr. Jacobs more and more.

He cleared his throat, his hand absentmindedly tapping the armrest of his chair. "His descriptions of their first meeting change with each telling. Patient seems to be an unreliable historian. I'm becoming more concerned that this whole relationship exists only in the patient's mind." The words lingered in the air, heavy with their implication.

Dr. Jacobs leaned forward again, resting his elbows on the desk, his fingers steepled as he stared at the recorder. "It's troubling," he admitted, his voice quieter now. "Gavin speaks with such conviction about Colton and the intensity of their connection, yet the inconsistencies and the fabrications suggest something else entirely. A man of his stature and confidence shouldn't feel this detached from reality."

His mind raced back to Gavin's recent sessions—how his mood would shift dramatically when talking about Eric, the calm and steady husband, compared to the almost frenzied excitement that colored his stories about Colton. The emotional detachment he showed toward his family, contrasted with the larger-than-life depiction of his lover, raised red flags that had only grown brighter in recent weeks.

Dr. Jacobs let out a slow breath, the sound barely audible in the quiet room. He knew this feeling all too well—the slow, creeping suspicion that something darker was hiding beneath the surface—something that had to be unraveled slowly and delicately, like a knot that tightened with each passing session.

"At this point," he said, his voice barely above a whisper, "I don't know what's real for Gavin. The discrepancies in his stories, the way he deflects when pressed—there's something he's not telling me. Or perhaps, something he can't tell me because he doesn't fully grasp it himself."

Dr. Jacobs leaned back in his chair, the weight of his own thoughts pressing heavily on his chest. He had worked with many patients who distorted reality to protect themselves from pain, but with Gavin, the lines between fact and fiction seemed especially blurred. And that terrified him—not just for Gavin, but for everyone in his life who might be affected by these delusions.

He glanced at the clock, its hands slowly ticking toward the end of the day, and closed his eyes, gathering his thoughts before speaking into the recorder once more. "I need to tread carefully. If Gavin is truly lost in a delusion, pulling him back might trigger something... *unpredictable*."

His hand hovered over the recorder, the weight of his responsibility settling in. He knew he needed to have more sessions with Gavin. Doing so would be critical, and he wasn't entirely sure how to proceed. But he had to.

"End of recording," Dr. Jacobs stated, pressing the stop button and sitting back.

For the first time in years, he wasn't sure if he was prepared for what was coming next.

Chapter 17

The streets buzzed with the usual city life—honking cars, distant chatter, and the steady rhythm of footsteps on the sidewalk. The tall glass buildings towered above, reflecting the midday sun, casting patterns of light and shadow across the pavement. Gavin moved through the crowd, his suit crisp and perfectly tailored, his leather shoes clicking against the concrete as he made his way toward the real estate office. The world around him felt like a background tune to his thoughts, which were still racing after the meeting with the travel agent and his plans for a surprise getaway with Eric.

He adjusted his cufflinks as he crossed the street, feeling a rare sense of control and satisfaction. Everything was aligning perfectly. The Fontina Beach House deal, the romantic trip for two—all of it felt like pieces falling into place. He was just a few blocks from the office when a sharp voice cut through the clamor of the city, stopping him in his tracks.

"Gavin!"

The sound of his name uttered with such force made him spin around. His heart skipped a beat when he saw Wesley Daniels standing on the corner of the street, his face flushed with anger, fists clenched at his sides. Gavin's eyes widened in brief surprise before he recovered, a cool smile curling on his lips.

"Well, if it isn't Wesley Daniels," Gavin said, his voice calm though his tone had an unmistakable hint of mockery. His gaze swept over Wesley—disheveled and tense, a stark contrast to Gavin's collected demeanor.

Wesley strode forward, the tension in his body evident with every step. "We're gonna talk," he demanded, his voice rough with barely restrained fury.

Gavin's eyes gleamed with amusement as he glanced at his watch, then back to Wesley. "I'm sorry, but I have a meeting I need to get to," he said smoothly, turning slightly as if to walk away.

"No!" Wesley's voice was louder now, stopping Gavin in his tracks again. "We're going to do this now." His face was flushed with impatience, his jaw set as he glared at Gavin. "You're going to stop avoiding me—my life has been a fucking train wreck since you passed through it."

Gavin turned back toward Wesley, raising an eyebrow. "Really? That's surprising," he said with such casualness. "I thought you'd been doing well all this time. I've seen some of your articles in the local magazine. You've really been making a name for yourself, haven't you?" He tilted his head slightly, his eyes gleaming. "See? I still follow your career even though we… stopped seeing each other."

Wesley's face twisted with anger, and he took a step closer, his fists still clenched. "We didn't see each other, Gavin!" he snapped, his voice shaking with barely contained rage.

Gavin shrugged, adjusting his cufflinks again, his gaze never leaving Wesley's. "Well, let's not get into that argument again," he said, his tone dismissive, as if the matter wasn't worth his time.

Wesley's eyes darkened with frustration, his hands shaking slightly as he ran them through his hair in agitation. "My husband Seth believed that crap about us having an affair," he hissed, his voice low and dangerous. "Do you have any idea what that did to my marriage?"

Gavin's expression remained calm. "Maybe because it was true," he said lightly.

Wesley's face contorted with disbelief, and he threw his hands up in the air in a gesture of utter exasperation. "Christ! We didn't, Gavin!" he shouted, drawing a few curious glances from passersby, though most of them quickly looked away, sensing the tension between the two men.

Gavin remained perfectly still, his face impassive as Wesley continued, his voice growing louder, more desperate. "It was all in that crazy, fucked-up head of yours."

The air between them crackled with unresolved tension. Gavin's face remained unreadable, but his eyes glinted with something almost imperceptible. His usual charm had taken on a slightly menacing edge, though he still looked every bit the confident, unbothered man he had always been.

Wesley, on the other hand, was unraveling before him. His anger, his desperation—it was all laid bare now. He had come to confront Gavin, to reclaim something of the life that had been shattered in the wake of their interactions, but as he stood there, face flushed, fists still clenched, he realized he was getting nowhere.

The city moved on around them, oblivious to the drama playing out on the sidewalk.

"This is ridiculous, what you're spewing," Gavin said, his voice cool and steady despite the rising frustration in his chest. His eyes were sharp as they met Wesley's, his expression showing condescending disbelief. "I don't understand why you feel the need to deny what we had."

Wesley's face twisted in anger, his jaw clenching so tightly that his teeth ground together. Without warning, he grabbed Gavin roughly by the arm, his fingers digging hard into the muscle of Gavin's upper tricep. The sudden burst of aggression was jarring, and for a split second, Gavin's calm façade faltered, his eyes widening in shock.

"Enough!" Wesley growled, his voice low and threatening. "You're going to fix what you destroyed. You're going to convince Seth that there was nothing between us."

Gavin's shock quickly turned to fury as he wrenched his arm free from Wesley's grip, stumbling back slightly as he recoiled from the force of the pull. His eyes flashed with anger, and his voice was sharp, cutting through the noise of the street like a blade. "You're hurting me!" he hissed, rubbing his arm where Wesley had grabbed him. His usually composed exterior now cracked, revealing a glimpse of vulnerability.

Wesley's breathing was heavy, his chest rising and falling with intensity. His face was red with fury, his hands shaking slightly as they hung at his sides. "I have nothing more to lose," he muttered through gritted teeth, his voice raw with desperation. There was a long pause, the tension between them thick enough to choke on.

Gavin stared at him, stunned by the force of Wesley's words. He could feel the intensity radiating from the man in front of him—this wasn't just anger anymore; it was something deeper, something more painful.

"I'm sorry," Gavin said slowly, his voice softer now, his tone shifting from sharp defensiveness to something resembling concern. "I didn't know you were so... *hurt*." His words were tentative, almost cautious, as if he was testing the waters to see how far he could push without setting Wesley off again.

Wesley's grip on his emotions loosened just slightly at Gavin's unexpected apology. He took a deep breath, the tension in his body easing as his posture softened. For the first time in the entire confrontation, there was something vulnerable in his eyes—something desperate and pleading. "Come with me to see him," Wesley said, his voice quieter now, almost pleading. "Tell him the truth."

Gavin shifted on his feet, glancing at the office building just behind him. The meeting he had been heading to suddenly felt like a lifeline, an excuse to distance himself from this messy altercation. "Yeah," he said, his voice light, as if trying to smooth over the situation. "I will. But it can't be this instant. I have to get to a meeting, and I can't be late." He gestured vaguely toward the building behind him, flashing Wesley a smile that was more polished than genuine.

Wesley's expression darkened again, suspicion creeping back into his eyes. "I'll wait," he said firmly, his voice hardening again.

Gavin let out a soft, practiced laugh, shaking his head as though the idea was absurd. "No, no, it'll be hours," he said, brushing the notion aside with a wave of his hand. "How about I meet you there? We can handle this later."

Wesley's eyes narrowed, the suspicion in his gaze deepening. "I can't trust you," he said flatly, his voice filled with a mixture of rage and resignation.

Gavin tilted his head slightly, his smile fading, but his tone remaining calm and reassuring. "Well, you're going to have to if you want me to go along with this," he said, his words measured as though he were negotiating a business deal.

Wesley let out a frustrated sigh, his hands once again clenching into fists at his sides. He could feel himself losing control of the situation, but he didn't know how to push Gavin further without causing a scene. "Ugh, fine!" Wesley spat, his tone exasperated. "I'll meet you back here at five."

Gavin's smile returned, smoother than ever, as though the tension between them had dissipated. "That works," he said with a shrug, as if this were nothing more than a minor inconvenience. He turned to walk away, but before he took his first step, Wesley pointed at him, his face twisted with a warning glare.

"Don't fuck with me, Gavin!" Wesley's voice was sharp, filled with an unmistakable edge of threat. "I know where to find you now."

Gavin took a long breath, then slowly turned back to face Wesley, his eyes narrowing slightly. But instead of engaging further, he simply rolled his eyes, the gesture dismissive and mocking. "Sure," he said with a nonchalant wave, his smile never fading. Without another word, he turned and walked into the office building, his posture as confident and composed as ever.

As the glass door closed behind him, cutting off the

chaotic noise of the street, Gavin felt the tension drain from his shoulders. The cool air of the lobby hit him, and he took a deep breath, composing himself as though nothing had happened. His mind was already shifting back to his work, to the meeting ahead. Wesley's outburst was already being pushed to the back of his mind, something to be dealt with later—if at all.

Outside, Wesley stood frozen on the sidewalk, his fists clenched and his body shaking with a mixture of anger and frustration. He watched Gavin disappear into the building, his heart pounding in his chest. He had been so close—so close to getting Gavin to face the truth, to fix the mess he had made of his life. But once again, Gavin had slipped away, leaving him standing there, helpless and furious.

Wesley's eyes darkened as he glared at the office building. "This isn't over," he muttered under his breath. He turned and walked away, his mind already churning with the next steps he would take.

Chapter 18

The late afternoon sun hung low in the sky, casting long shadows across the street as Gavin strolled along, his phone held loosely in his hand. The sounds of the city surrounded him—the rumble of traffic, the distant chatter of pedestrians, and the occasional honk of a car horn. His day had been long but successful, and now, as he made his way through the familiar streets, he allowed his mind to wander, his thoughts shifting between his recent real estate triumph and his plans with Eric.

Suddenly, his phone buzzed in his hand, the screen lighting up with an all-too-familiar number. A strange feeling crept over him, but he pressed the answer button, raising the phone to his ear.

"Hello?" Gavin said, his voice casual as he continued to walk, weaving through the foot traffic.

There was a brief pause, and then a voice he hadn't heard in a while slipped through the line, smooth and low.

"You look so damn sexy walking on the street, right by that hot dog vendor. I can't help but think about all the dirty things I'd do to you," Colton said, in a low, sultry voice.

Gavin spun around, realizing he did just, in fact, pass a hot dog stand. "How did you know I just walked by that stand? Are you following me?"

"I don't have to see you to know what you're doing," Colton's voice purred, dripping with that familiar, unsettling confidence.

Gavin's heart skipped a beat, though he quickly masked his surprise with a slight laugh, leaning into his playful side. "Where are you?" he asked, his tone almost flirtatious, though anxiety crept in.

Colton chuckled on the other end, the sound unsettling in its familiarity. "Oh, Gavin," he said, his voice soft but with an undercurrent of something darker. "I don't have to be near you to know exactly what you're up to. You know you can't keep secrets from me."

Gavin slowed his pace, his eyes darting around the street, scanning the faces of the passersby, though none of them seemed to pay him any mind. "Now you're scaring me," he said, a slight edge to his voice as he glanced over his shoulder.

"Oh, come on," Colton teased, the playful tone still present but now laced with something more sinister. "You know you miss me. You miss *us*."

Gavin let out a short laugh, shaking his head as if the very idea was absurd. "What is it you think you know?" he asked, though his voice wasn't quite as steady as before.

"I know you miss me," Colton replied, his words slow and deliberate, like he was savoring each syllable.

"Wrong," Gavin shot back, his voice a little too sharp. He quickened his pace, his shoes tapping louder against the pavement. But the unease gnawed at him now, tightening in his chest.

Colton's voice didn't waver. "I know you miss what we had," he continued, and this time, there was a faint amusement in his tone as though he knew exactly how to get under Gavin's skin.

Gavin laughed again, though it felt forced. "Wrong again," he said, his voice strained with deflection. His eyes continued to dart around, the creeping sensation that Colton was watching him becoming harder to ignore.

There was a pause on the line, a silence that stretched just long enough to make Gavin's skin crawl. And then Colton spoke again, his voice low, predatory. "You have the sexiest ass in town, like I've always said," he purred. "I'm really digging the blue blazer."

Gavin stopped dead in his tracks, his breath catching

in his throat. His heart raced as he glanced down at his clothes—his navy-blue blazer, perfectly fitted, crisp against his white shirt. His eyes scanned the street again, but this time with an intensity bordering on panic. "Okay... Where are you?" Gavin's voice dropped, now strained with a tension he couldn't hide.

Colton laughed softly, the sound sending a chill down Gavin's spine. "Right here," he said, his voice steady, certain. "Right in front of you. Right where I always am."

Gavin's eyes shot forward, and there, standing across the street, leaning casually against a lamppost, was Colton. He hung up the phone just as their eyes locked, a slow smirk spreading across his face. Colton pushed himself off the post and started walking toward Gavin, slipping his phone into his pocket with the same smooth confidence that Gavin remembered all too well.

Gavin stared, his breath catching in his chest, his mind racing. Before he could think of something to say, Colton was right there in front of him, reaching out to grab his hand.

Colton's grip was firm but not forceful as he started walking, pulling Gavin along with him. "What do you think you're doing?" Gavin asked, his voice sharp, though he didn't pull away immediately.

"Kidnapping you," Colton replied, his tone so nonchalant it almost sounded like a joke.

Gavin huffed, finally pulling back slightly but not quite letting go. "I don't have time to be kidnapped again by you. Hasn't this charade gone on long enough? Where are you taking me?"

Colton glanced at him sideways, his smirk widening. "Somewhere special."

Gavin rolled his eyes, though his pulse was still racing. "Colton..." he said, his voice a mix of exasperation and reluctance.

Colton's grip on his hand tightened just slightly as they

continued walking. "I have to show you something," he said, his voice softer now, almost pleading. "I want to prove to you that I wasn't a complete asshole. Please. Come with me?"

Gavin hesitated, his mind a whirl of conflicting emotions. Colton had always been like this—smooth, charming, manipulative. He knew it was dangerous to indulge him, to let this continue. But the curiosity won over his logic, and part of him—some small, reckless part—wanted to see what Colton had in mind.

"Fine," Gavin said, sighing dramatically. "But you have one hour, tops."

Colton grinned, clearly pleased. "That's all I need," he said, giving Gavin's hand a light squeeze before leading him further down the street.

As they walked, the tension between them hung thick in the air, unspoken words lingering just beneath the surface. Gavin's mind raced, his instincts telling him to pull away, to turn back. But something kept him moving forward, following Colton through the busy streets as if the city around them didn't even exist until he was able to hail a cab.

Colton opened the back door of the taxi, ushering Gavin in. Closing the door behind him, Colton leaned forward to whisper to the driver the surprise destination he was taking Gavin to. The driver soon took off.

The city lights flickered as the cab made its way through the narrow streets, weaving between buildings with the ease of a well-practiced dance. Gavin sat in the backseat next to Colton, the seat leather cool against his skin as the faint roar of the car engine filled the silence between them. The city outside was a blur of neon lights, shop windows, and the occasional flash of pedestrians crossing the street, but Gavin's thoughts were entirely elsewhere. His mind was racing, unable to fully grasp the whirlwind of the last few minutes.

Colton had dragged him into this—literally—his grip

firm but somehow reassuring, and now they were headed to who knows where. Gavin wasn't sure what to expect, but something in Colton's demeanor had shifted. There was a weight behind his words and the way he looked at Gavin. It made him feel unsettled but curious.

The cab soon pulled up to the all-too-familiar art gallery, and Colton shot out of it, pulling Gavin along behind him. They soon entered the building.

Inside, the gallery was bathed in soft, warm light, casting a golden glow over the clean concrete floors. Paintings hung on the walls, each piece carefully lit to emphasize its importance, and the air was filled with the faint scent of oil paint and varnish. The space was quiet, almost reverent, as if each work of art demanded absolute attention.

Colton led Gavin deeper into the gallery, not saying a word. His hand lightly rested on the small of Gavin's back, guiding him through the maze of artwork. Finally, they stopped before a large canvas, and Gavin felt his breath catch in his throat.

There, hanging on the wall before him, was a painting of himself—naked. The brushstrokes were soft yet deliberate, capturing every curve, every shadow, with an intimacy that took Gavin's breath away. His body was depicted in repose, reclining as if in a dream, his skin bathed in soft light. The details were exquisite—the way the muscles of his body were rendered, the slight arch of his neck, the delicate interplay of light and shadow across his skin.

It was... beautiful.

Gavin stood there, speechless, his eyes wide as he took it all in. He had never seen himself like this—so vulnerable, so exposed, yet somehow... *perfect*. The painting captured him in a way that felt almost surreal, as if Colton had seen a side of him that he hadn't known existed.

"I... I don't know what to say," Gavin whispered, his voice barely audible in the vast silence of the gallery. His heart was pounding in his chest, and he couldn't tear his eyes away from the painting.

Colton stepped closer, his presence almost overwhelming. He grabbed Gavin by the wrist, pulling him gently into a nearby side hallway, where they were hidden from view. The walls here were lined with smaller, more intimate works, but Gavin barely noticed them. His mind was still reeling from the painting.

Colton cupped Gavin's cheek with his hand, his thumb brushing lightly across Gavin's skin in an almost tender gesture. "I really fucking miss you," Colton whispered, his voice low and raw with emotion. His eyes locked onto Gavin's, filled with a mixture of longing and something darker, something more primal. "Come on…"

Before Gavin could say anything, Colton's grip tightened, and he pulled him closer, the heat of their bodies almost unbearable in the narrow hallway. There was an electricity between them, a current that Gavin hadn't felt in so long—something dangerous, intoxicating.

Without waiting for a response, Colton's hand slid down to Gavin's wrist again, this time more firmly, as if refusing to let him slip away. He dragged Gavin out of the gallery, into the cool afternoon air, and down the street toward his apartment. Gavin followed, his mind clouded with emotions he couldn't quite place—part of him wanting to pull away, another part of him not wanting to at all.

When they arrived at Colton's building, Colton led Gavin inside, up the stairs, and into his loft.

As soon as the door clicked shut behind them, Colton turned to Gavin, his eyes dark with intensity. He moved in close, his hand slipping up Gavin's arm, resting on his shoulder as if silently asking permission for what came next.

Gavin's heart raced while his mind was a whirlwind of conflicting thoughts. Part of him knew he should walk away—that whatever this was between them, it was dangerous and unstable. But another part of him, the part that had been drawn to Colton from the very beginning, couldn't resist.

"Colton..." Gavin started, his voice barely above a whisper, but Colton cut him off.

"Strip down for me, Gavin," Colton commanded in a low, husky voice. Gavin, his heart pounding in his chest, obeyed without hesitation. He slowly unbuttoned his crisp white shirt, revealing his toned chest and washboard abs. Next, he unbuckled his belt, unbuttoned his tailored slacks, and let them fall to the floor. As he stood before Colton in nothing but his tight black boxer briefs, Gavin could feel his cock twitching with excitement.

"Very good," Colton purred, moving closer to Gavin. "Now, it's time for me to show you what it means to truly submit."

Colton reached out and gently ran his fingers along the outline of Gavin's bulging erection through his boxer briefs. Gavin let out a soft moan, his body trembling with desire. Colton then hooked his fingers into the waistband of Gavin's underwear and yanked them down, exposing Gavin's swollen, throbbing dick.

Kneeling before Gavin, Colton took his cock into his mouth, swirling his tongue around the sensitive head. Gavin's knees buckled, and he let out a deep, hoarse groan. Colton continued to pleasure Gavin with his expert mouth, bobbing his head up and down, taking Gavin deeper into his throat with each thrust.

After a few minutes of intense oral stimulation, Colton stood up and turned Gavin around, pressing his chest against the cool glass of the floor-to-ceiling windows overlooking the city. Gavin's heart raced as he felt Colton's strong hands roughly grabbing at his ass cheeks, spreading them apart.

"You're going to take every inch of my cock, do you understand?" Colton growled, his voice dripping with lust.

Without waiting for a response, Colton leaned down

and buried his face between Gavin's round, firm ass cheeks. Gavin couldn't help but release a series of high-pitched moans as Colton's tongue worked its magic, lapping at his tight, pink hole.

"Oh, fuck, Colton," Gavin whimpered, his voice barely a whisper. "I want your cock inside me so bad."

Colton chuckled darkly, his voice laced with desire. "Not yet. I want to make sure you're nice and ready for me."

Colton continued to eat out Gavin's ass, his tongue darting in and out of his tight entrance. Gavin's moans grew louder and more desperate with each passing second. Finally, after what felt like an eternity of pure ecstasy, Colton stood up and spat into his hand, using the saliva to lube up Gavin's hole.

"Now, it's time for you to get on your knees and suck my cock like the good little slut you are," Colton commanded, his voice dripping with dominance.

Gavin obeyed without hesitation, dropping down onto his hands and knees. Colton stepped forward, positioning the thick, pulsating head of his cock right in front of Gavin's eager mouth. Gavin wasted no time in wrapping his lips around Colton's shaft, taking him deep into his throat.

Colton groaned with pleasure, his hands tangled in Gavin's hair as he began to thrust his hips back and forth, fucking Gavin's mouth with reckless abandon. Gavin's eyes watered, but he didn't dare pull away. Instead, he reached down between his legs and began to stroke his own aching cock.

After a few minutes of intense oral pleasure, Colton pulled his cock out of Gavin's mouth with a wet, sloppy pop. He then grabbed Gavin by the hips and roughly adjusted him so that he was perfectly behind Gavin.

"Now, it's time for me to claim you and that ass I *own*," Colton growled, positioning the swollen head of his cock right at Gavin's entrance. Gavin let out a loud gasp as Colton thrust his hips forward, driving his thick, throbbing shaft deep inside Gavin's tight, willing hole.

"Holy fuck, Colton," Gavin moaned, his voice filled with pleasure and pain. "Give it to me harder!"

Colton obliged, his hands gripping onto Gavin's hips as he began to fuck him with wild, unrestrained fervor. Gavin's body shook with each powerful thrust, his own cock bouncing up and down with each passing second.

"You like that, don't you, my little fuck toy?" Colton sneered, his voice dripping with sadistic pleasure. "You love having my big, fucking thick cock pounding away at your tight little ass."

Gavin could only moan and whimper in response, his body trembling with pleasure and pain. Colton continued to fuck him without restraint, his hips slamming into Gavin's round, firm ass cheeks with a loud, wet smack.

As the intensity of their passionate lovemaking reached its fever pitch, Colton could feel his own orgasm building up deep within his loins. With a loud, primal roar, he thrust his hips forward one final time, driving his cock as deep inside Gavin's ass as far as it would go.

"Oh, fuck, Gavin," Colton groaned, his voice filled with pure ecstasy. "I'm gonna cum in you."

With that, Colton exploded deep within Gavin's tight, willing hole, filling him up with his warm, thick seed. Gavin let out a loud, guttural groan as he felt Colton's cock twitching and pulsating deep inside him, emptying its load.

Finally, after what felt like an eternity of pure bliss, Colton slowly pulled his cock out of Gavin's ass, his shaft still hard and coated in a mixture of sweat, pre-cum, and their combined fluids. Gavin collapsed onto the floor, his body trembling with exhaustion and pure, unbridled pleasure.

They just lay on the ground, panting to catch their breath. The wooden floor beneath them felt cool against their skin, contrasting with the heat of their bodies. Gavin lay nestled in Colton's arms, his chest rising and falling with deep, contented breaths. The room around them was dim, the late afternoon sun casting a soft glow through the loft's large windows, illuminating the paint-splattered canvases leaning haphazardly against the walls. It was a chaotic space, but right now, there was a calm between them, a silence that felt comfortable, if not a little surreal.

They had been lying there for what felt like an hour, not speaking, just holding onto each other, the weight of their recent intimacy settling in the air around them. Colton's fingers traced lazy circles on Gavin's shoulder, his touch light, almost absentminded, but still grounding. Gavin's eyes were half-closed, his mind somewhere between relaxation and thought, still processing everything.

Finally, Gavin shifted slightly, his stomach grumbling in protest as reality crept back in. "We should probably get up," he murmured, his voice low and a bit hoarse from the exertion.

Colton chuckled softly, his breath warm against Gavin's ear. "You're right," he said, though he made no immediate move to let go. He tightened his arms around Gavin for just a moment longer, as if reluctant to break the spell of their quiet time together. "But I'm not in a rush."

Gavin smiled, the sound of Colton's heart beating beneath him soothing, but his stomach rumbled again, more insistently this time. "I'm starving," he admitted, finally pulling away and sitting up, his hand running through his tousled hair. He glanced over at Colton with a wry smile. "All that energy we just spent... I need food."

Colton grinned, his eyes sparkling with amusement as he sat up as well, stretching his arms above his head. "I guess that's fair," he said, yawning slightly. "Okay, let's get dressed and find something to eat."

They both rose, the sound of the wooden floor creaking beneath their feet as they dressed in a comfortable silence. Gavin pulled on his clothes, glancing around the room once more. Colton's loft always had a certain charm—messy but lived in, like a place where creativity happened organically, without the need for structure or order.

Once they were both dressed, they stepped outside into the early evening air. The city was alive with the sounds of people moving about, the streets busy with vendors selling their wares. The smell of sizzling food filled the air as they made their way toward a street vendor market, the bright colors of the stalls standing out against the dull gray of the city streets.

The market was bustling, the atmosphere lively with the chatter of people ordering food and perusing the various stands. The smells were intoxicating—grilled meats, fresh spices, and the rich aroma of street food wafting from every corner. Gavin felt his stomach grumble in response, and he exchanged a glance with Colton, who was grinning like a kid at a carnival.

"Alright, what are we feeling?" Colton asked, scanning the vendors. "Something greasy or something healthy?"

"Greasy," Gavin said without hesitation, his eyes landing on a stall selling grilled kebabs and fried dumplings. "After what we just did, I deserve something good."

They approached the stall, and Gavin ordered a skewer of spicy grilled lamb while Colton opted for dumplings, the crispy golden pockets steaming as they were handed over. The vendor smiled as he passed the food to them, and Gavin's mouth watered at the sight.

They found a small corner to stand and eat, the sounds of the city around them almost comforting in their familiarity. Gavin took a bite of the lamb, the spices exploding on his tongue, the meat tender and perfectly cooked. He let out a satisfied groan, wiping his mouth with the back of his hand. "This is exactly what I needed," he said, grinning at Colton.

Colton took a bite of his dumpling, nodding in agreement. "We should do this more often," he said, his voice casual but with an underlying warmth. There was something easy about being with Colton, something that felt… *free*.

But as they stood there, eating and laughing, Gavin's eyes caught sight of something—or rather, someone—that made his blood run cold.

Just across the market, walking slowly past a row of stalls, was Eric. And beside him, holding his hand and chatting excitedly, was Ashton. They were shopping, laughing together, completely unaware of Gavin's presence—or his current situation.

Panic surged through Gavin like a bolt of electricity, his heart hammering in his chest. He whipped his head around to Colton, who was mid-bite, completely oblivious to the danger looming just across the street.

"Colton," Gavin hissed, grabbing his arm with sudden urgency. "We need to get out of here. Now."

Colton looked at him, startled by the shift in Gavin's tone. "What? Why?"

Gavin's eyes darted back to where Eric and Ashton were browsing a nearby stall, his stomach twisting into knots. "Eric and Ashton—they're right there," he whispered, his voice strained with panic. "I can't let them see us like this. Please, we need to go."

Colton's eyes widened slightly, his gaze following Gavin's line of sight. He seemed frozen, but then his lips curled into a smirk, amused by the situation. "Oh, come on," he said, but Gavin's panic was real, and Colton quickly sobered up. "Okay, okay."

Without wasting another second, Gavin yanked Colton into a narrow alleyway that ran behind one of the vendor stalls. The walls of the alley were grimy, and the smell of old food and wet pavement was strong in the air, but Gavin didn't care. He pressed his back against the wall, his breathing shallow as he peeked around the corner to make sure Eric hadn't spotted them.

Colton leaned against the wall beside him, chuckling softly as he wiped his hands on his jeans. "Well, that was close," he teased, his eyes glittering with mischief.

Gavin shot him a look, still trying to catch his breath. "You're enjoying this way too much," he muttered, shaking his head. But despite the current tension, he couldn't help but laugh, the absurdity of the situation catching up with him. "God, we could've been caught."

Colton grinned, his eyes locking onto Gavin's. "But we weren't," he said, stepping closer and resting a hand on Gavin's shoulder, his touch familiar and warm.

The fear and panic faded away, soon replaced by the pull between them. Colton leaned in, his lips brushing against Gavin's, soft at first, then more insistent. Gavin responded, his arms wrapping around Colton's waist as they kissed, hidden away in the alley.

After a few seconds, they pulled back, both of them breathless and laughing. The coast was clear—Eric and Ashton had moved on, none the wiser.

Gavin exhaled, his heart finally starting to slow. "Okay," he said, smiling, as he pushed Colton lightly. "We should part ways before I have another heart attack."

Colton laughed, nodding in agreement. "Alright, alright. But you have to admit, that was kind of fun."

Gavin rolled his eyes but smiled anyway, the tension in his chest finally easing. "Yeah, sure. Let's not make a habit of it."

With one last lingering look, they stepped out of the alley and went their separate ways, the market buzzing around them as if nothing had happened.

Chapter 19

The usual sounds of agents talking and constant ringtones going off on phones at the real estate office filled Gavin's ears as he sat at his desk, fingers skimming across the keyboard. The familiar rhythm of real estate reports, emails, and phone calls made the day feel predictable—something he usually craved. Gavin found himself lost in his work. Everything was just as it should be.

Then, his phone rang, breaking the calm. He glanced at the screen, seeing the familiar number flash—*Dr. Jacobs*.

Gavin hesitated, his hand hovering over the phone before he picked it up. "Hello?" he answered, trying to keep his tone casual, though a part of him already knew where this conversation was headed.

"Gavin," Dr. Jacobs' voice came through, calm but insistent. "I know you said you were done with me, but I highly implore you to reconsider and come back to see me."

Gavin sighed, leaning back in his chair. His eyes fixated on the city outside, his mind racing through the past weeks—Colton, Eric, everything he'd been juggling. But he wasn't about to let Dr. Jacobs get under his skin again. "I'm fine," Gavin replied, his tone dismissive. "Really, I don't need it."

Dr. Jacobs didn't miss a beat. "I have an opening today at 4:00 pm. I think it would be beneficial for you to come in, even just to talk."

Gavin rubbed his forehead, a soft sigh escaping his lips. "Thanks, but no, really. I don't need it," he said, trying to keep his voice steady. He could feel the tension building, but he wasn't ready to face it yet—not in front of Dr. Jacobs.

Before Dr. Jacobs could respond, a loud voice echoed down the hallway, interrupting the office's relative calm.

Gavin stiffened, hearing the unmistakable sound of Wesley Daniels shouting.

"Gavin! Gavin! I need to see him now! I'm through with this!"

Gavin's heart raced as the sound of Wesley's voice grew closer, cutting through the professional atmosphere of the office like a blade. He could already picture Wesley storming down the hall, his face red with anger.

Dr. Jacobs, still on the line, seemed to hear the commotion. "Gavin, seriously. I'll leave the timeslot open no matter what. Please come in."

But Gavin wasn't listening anymore. His attention was entirely focused on the chaos brewing just outside his office. "I've got to go," he muttered into the phone, hanging up quickly before Dr. Jacobs could argue further.

As he stood and made his way to the door, the tension in the air grew palpable. Wesley's voice was unmistakable now, sharp and angry, as he continued to shout down the hall. "I need to see him now! This ends today!"

Gavin opened the door to see Wesley standing in the middle of the hallway, glaring at the reception desk. His face was flushed with rage, his fists clenched at his sides. The receptionist looked bewildered, trying to calm him down, but it was clear Wesley wasn't having it.

Gavin stepped forward, keeping his voice calm. "Oh? Were you looking for me, Wesley?"

Wesley spun around, his eyes flashing with sarcasm and anger. "No," he spat, his voice dripping with venom. "I want to buy a fucking condo."

Gavin smiled faintly, doing his best to remain composed. He noticed Dwight, the security guard, approaching from the other end of the hall, concern etched on his face. "Thanks, Dwight," Gavin said, holding up a hand. "I'm good."

He then returned his attention back to Wesley. "Let's not do this here, please."

But Wesley wasn't backing down. His face twisted with impatience as he pointed a finger at Gavin. "No! I'm done with trusting you. We do this now!" His voice was sharp, unrelenting. "I'm not leaving sight of you until you speak to Seth. We were supposed to meet two days ago, and you never showed up. You obviously didn't come to work yesterday because I was here. I waited all day, Gavin. All day! I am through taking you at your so-called *word*. Let's go now!"

Gavin took a deep breath, glancing briefly at the other staff who were watching the confrontation with thinly veiled interest. His jaw tightened, but he kept his voice steady. "Wesley," he said, his tone measured, "we can talk about this privately. But you need to calm down."

"Calm down?" Wesley's voice cracked with disbelief. "I've given you enough chances to fix this, Gavin. Enough lies. Enough excuses. We're doing this now."

Gavin's mind raced as he tried to navigate the situation, the tension between them thickening with every word. He knew Wesley wouldn't leave without a dispute, but the last thing he wanted was to drag this out in front of the entire office.

"Fine," Gavin said finally, his voice softening as he took a step closer. "We'll talk. But not here."

Wesley glared at him, his eyes narrowing. "You're not getting away this time."

"I'm not trying to," Gavin replied calmly, glancing at Dwight, who was still hovering nearby. "Just give me a minute to wrap up, and we'll go."

Wesley's nostrils flared, but soon, he nodded curtly, admitting he had no other say. "You have five minutes," he muttered, folding his arms tightly across his chest.

Gavin turned, walking back into his office, the weight of the situation pressing down on him. He wasn't sure how much longer he could keep this juggling act going, but one thing was clear—Wesley was done waiting.

Gavin and Wesley stepped out of the elevator and into the plush hallway of a luxury high-rise. The walls were adorned with expensive, abstract art, and the thick carpet beneath their feet muted the sounds of their footsteps. The air smelled faintly of expensive cologne and cedarwood, a distinct scent that seemed to permeate through these kinds of swanky buildings. Gavin cast a sideways glance at Wesley, who looked tense but determined, his jaw set as they approached the door of Seth's apartment.

The building was impressive, with high ceilings and floor-to-ceiling windows that offered breathtaking views of the city skyline. Even from the hallway, you could feel the weight of money in every detail, from the bronze light fixtures to the marble accents. Gavin had always been impressed by places like this, but today, the grandeur felt like a backdrop to the confrontation that was about to unfold.

As they reached the door, Wesley knocked firmly, his knuckles rapping against the heavy wood with purpose. He glanced at Gavin, his face rigid with expectation.

"I expect you to tell him the truth," Wesley said quietly, but there was an edge to his voice. The way he stared at Gavin told him there was no room for games today.

Gavin sighed, already feeling the weight of the impending argument settling on his chest. "I'll tell your husband whatever you want me to tell him," he replied, his voice flat with resignation.

Wesley shook his head, his eyes narrowing. "No, Gavin. I want you to tell him the *truth*."

Before Gavin could respond, the door opened. Seth stood there, dressed casually in a well-tailored shirt and jeans, his expression immediately darkening when he saw them. He looked healthier than Gavin had expected—his eyes sharp, his posture upright—but the hostility radiating from him was palpable.

"What the hell is this?" Seth muttered, glaring between the two of them. He moved to shut the door, but Wesley quickly stepped forward, blocking the entrance.

"Please, Seth," Wesley said, his voice pleading but firm. "Just give me five minutes. Hear me out."

Seth's gaze slid over to Gavin, his eyes narrowing further. "What the hell is *he* doing here?" he spat, his tone filled with contempt.

Wesley shot Gavin a look as if telling him to stay quiet for now. "Just listen to what he has to say," Wesley urged, his voice tight with desperation.

But Seth wasn't having it. "I don't want to hear anything that fucking whore has to say," he snarled, his words cutting through the air like a knife.

Gavin flinched inwardly, but kept his face composed. He could feel the tension rolling off both Seth and Wesley, the room practically vibrating with it. Wesley nudged Gavin hard, a clear signal for him to start talking.

"Tell him the truth, damnit!" Wesley demanded, his voice sharp.

Gavin exhaled slowly, trying to steady his nerves. He met Seth's gaze, feeling the weight of the situation. "It's not what you think... about Wesley and me," Gavin began, his voice quiet but steady. "We met at work. We had lunch a few times—"

"Oh, really?" Seth cut him off, his voice dripping with sarcasm. He turned to Wesley. "Lunch? I thought you said he was a complete stranger."

Wesley quickly interjected, shaking his head. "No! We didn't have lunch. We met at the coffee shop. Making small talk at a lunch counter doesn't qualify as *having lunch*."

Seth's eyes darted between the two of them, his indignation bubbling up. "Seriously? Get your fucking story straight."

Wesley's face was red, his voice growing desperate. "I swear to you, Seth, that's all that happened. We chatted a couple of times, and the next thing I know, Gavin is blowing our lives apart."

He turned to Gavin again, his eyes pleading. "Tell him the truth, Gavin!"

Gavin sighed, his gaze darting to Seth. He could feel the room closing in around him, the walls of this luxurious apartment somehow making everything feel smaller, more intense. "Wesley and I didn't have an affair," he said slowly, the words hanging in the air. "I wanted to, but… he wouldn't."

Seth stared at him, his face twisted in a mixture of disbelief and disgust. "Then what about all the phone calls? The emails? The dirty gifts that kept showing up?"

Wesley's eyes blazed with anger. "He did all that! Unprovoked! This whole thing is in his crazy head!"

Seth's gaze bore into Gavin, his voice low and dangerous. "Is that true?"

Gavin swallowed, the weight of the truth heavy on his shoulders. He nodded reluctantly. "Yes."

Seth's face contorted with rage and disbelief. "You really didn't know him?" he asked, his voice quieter now but no less angry.

Gavin shook his head, tears prickling at the edges of his eyes. "No…"

Seth's anger boiled over, his voice sharp and accusatory. "So, you made the whole thing up? You blew our lives apart because of some stupid, fucked-up fantasy? Is that it? What kind of sick fucking creep are you!?"

Gavin's composure finally cracked, his irritation bubbling to the surface. "I *cared* about Wesley," he snapped, his voice rising. "I showed up here now because I care about Wesley, which is more than I can say for you." His words came out faster now, fueled by frustration and rage. "You didn't even care enough to fight for your marriage. You just ran out on him the very first chance you got."

The room was silent, the air thick with tension. Seth's face was a mixture of shock and fury, and Wesley stood there, frozen, caught between the two of them.

Gavin turned to Wesley, his face hard. "There. I did it. Are you happy now?" he asked, his voice bitter. "I said what you wanted me to say, and frankly, I don't think this stuck-up bitch is worth it."

Wesley's eyes widened, but before he could respond, Gavin was already turning toward the door. "Now leave me the fuck alone," Gavin muttered, storming out of the apartment.

Behind him, Seth slammed his front door shut with a force that echoed through the hallway. Gavin didn't look back, his mind racing as he walked briskly down the hall, the weight of the confrontation still heavy on his shoulders. He could feel the adrenaline pumping through his veins, but all he wanted was to be anywhere but here.

As the door clicked shut, Wesley stood frozen in the hallway, his hands shaking slightly, his mind trying to process what had just happened. He glanced at the door, then back down the hall where Gavin had disappeared, just stunned. It was undoubtedly the most bizarre situation Wesley had encountered in his entire life. And that was saying something considering he was a journalist and thought he had seen it all.

Chapter 20

Gavin stormed out of Seth's high-rise, the heavy door slamming shut behind him with a loud thud. The lobby of the building gleamed under bright chandeliers, a stark contrast to the chaos swirling inside his mind. He was flabbergasted, replaying the conversation with Wesley and Seth over and over again. The altercation had spiraled out of control, leaving him feeling raw, exposed, and angrier than before. Every step he took echoed through the pristine space, the marble floor cold beneath his feet as he headed toward the building's grand exit.

The afternoon air hit him as soon as he stepped outside, the city alive with the usual hustle and bustle. The sun was dipping lower in the sky, casting long shadows across the street. Gavin pulled his coat tighter around him, trying to shake off the remnants of the argument, but the words clung to him, making his skin crawl. He needed to clear his head.

As he walked down the street, heading nowhere in particular, he almost collided with a woman coming from the opposite direction. Startled, he took a step back and blinked in recognition. It was someone from the yoga studio—a participant.

"Oh! Sorry," Gavin muttered, trying to sidestep her, but she seemed intent on speaking.

"You were at yoga that day, weren't you? The day Jason was killed?" the woman asked, her eyes narrowing as she took him in. She had an air of authority about her—calm but direct. "I remember you. I was also there that day. I manage our studio and the company."

Gavin froze, the color draining from his face as he stared

at her. His mind scrambled for a response, but he couldn't find the right words. "Oh god. Right. What a freak accident," he finally managed, his voice sounding far less steady than he intended.

The woman didn't seem convinced. She crossed her arms, her gaze unflinching. "I'm not sure the police think so," she said, her tone sharp. "They've been all over the cliffside and the studio, looking for clues, evidence. The whole thing is a nightmare for my business. They're definitely suspicious of it being more than just an accident."

Gavin's heart began to race. His hands felt clammy, and he clenched them into fists to stop the trembling. "I hadn't heard about that," he replied, forcing a casual tone, but it was clear the conversation was headed somewhere he didn't want to go.

The yoga manager tilted her head, studying him closely. "But really, weren't you the guy I saw when I left? You were still there, right?"

Gavin's pulse quickened, panic rising in his throat. He could feel her eyes on him, piercing through the façade he'd carefully constructed. "I don't think so," he said quickly, shaking his head. "But I wasn't fully focused that day."

The woman's brows furrowed, her expression skeptical. "Maybe I'm wrong, but I could've sworn I saw you being the last one to leave. Did you see anyone else there after class?"

Gavin felt the walls closing in. His chest tightened as the memories of that day resurfaced—Jason on the cliffside, the silence after it happened. He swallowed hard, trying to keep his voice steady. "Like I told the police, I really didn't notice. I'm so sorry, but I'm running late for a meeting." He flashed her a tight smile before quickly brushing past her, his steps hurried.

As Gavin made his way down the street, his heart pounded in his chest, his mind racing. The encounter had rattled him far more than he cared to admit. The police were investigating, the yoga studio was involved, and now, this woman remembered seeing him there. He could feel everything slipping out of control.

His feet carried him faster, almost of their own accord, until he found himself standing outside Dr. Jacobs' office building. The familiar sight of the brick façade, the neatly trimmed shrubs lining the sidewalk, and the large bay window overlooking the street stopped him in his tracks. He hadn't intended to come here, but somehow, after everything, this was precisely where he needed to be.

Taking a deep breath, Gavin pulled open the door and stepped inside. The quiet of the office lobby was a stark contrast to the chaos in his mind. He needed to talk. He needed to figure this out.

Dr. Jacobs was his only option now.

Gavin sat in Dr. Jacobs' office. The soft ticking of the clock on the wall felt louder today, almost intrusive. He hadn't intended to come back, but after everything with Wesley, Seth, and the strange encounter with the yoga studio manager, he felt cornered. And when people felt cornered, they sought an escape. But Gavin wasn't quite sure what he was escaping from now.

"I'm glad you decided to come back, Gavin," Dr. Jacobs said gently, his voice breaking the silence.

Gavin shifted in his chair, his fingers nervously playing with the edge of his coat. "Well, I'm not sure why I'm here," he admitted, sounding more vulnerable than he intended. "But lately, I've been feeling bombarded by so many things. I thought maybe talking with you could help."

Dr. Jacobs nodded, leaning forward slightly. "I'm thrilled you made it," he said, his tone warm but tinged with concern.

"I think it's important that we talk some more."

Gavin raised an eyebrow, feeling a wave of suspicion rise within him. "Really? What did you want to talk about?" he asked, his voice slightly defensive.

Dr. Jacobs folded his hands, his gaze steady on Gavin. "About your relationships, Gavin," he said softly. "Especially the one with Colton. I'm concerned... that your life isn't on strong enough footing to keep you from drifting back to him."

Gavin blinked, caught off guard by the directness of the statement. He hesitated, then let out a sigh. "Well, the truth is, yes... I have seen him," Gavin confessed, his voice lowering. "Just the other day, he contacted me. He brought me to see a painting at his gallery. It was... *magnificent*. It was of me. Of my body."

Dr. Jacobs remained quiet, absorbing Gavin's words. "I see," he said slowly, leaning back in his chair. "Hmm... Sometimes, our view of relationships isn't completely realistic. We become so emotionally needy that we create fantasies or false connections, and we believe they are real."

Gavin frowned, his body tensing at Dr. Jacobs' words. "What's not real? Do you think I'm not real or something? Do you think Colton is not real?" he asked, his voice rising slightly, a note of indignation creeping in.

Dr. Jacobs shook his head gently. "No, I know you're real, Gavin. And I believe Colton is real as well," he said carefully. "I just wonder if your love affair with him is real."

Gavin stared at him, his heart pounding in his chest, a mixture of fury and disbelief bubbling up. "That's crazy!" he snapped. "You think I'm imagining my relationship with Colton? Is that what you're saying?"

Dr. Jacobs kept his voice calm and steady. "That's what I'm *asking*," he clarified. "Often, when things aren't going well in our primary relationships, we create an escape—a connection that gives us what we feel we're missing. For instance, you want to go to Paris, but you can't, so you paint a picture of it on your wall. A mural, a scene meant to trick your mind…"

Gavin's eyes flashed with recognition. "*Trompe L'Oeil*," he said abruptly, the word rolling off his tongue like a challenge.

Dr. Jacobs blinked, caught off guard. "What?" he asked, his brow furrowing in confusion.

"Trompe L'Oeil," Gavin repeated. "That's what it's called. The illusion of the eye in art. A two-dimensional figure appearing so realistic, it's believable."

Dr. Jacobs seemed to consider this, then nodded slowly. "Well, you understand that concept, don't you?" he said quietly. "You did it when you were young."

Gavin's face hardened, his jaw clenching. "You can't be serious," he said, his voice now edged with anger. "I did not imagine those men when I was young. You're defending my father and his actions, and now you're calling me a liar about the sick shit I went through growing up? What kind of therapist are you?"

Dr. Jacobs leaned forward, his voice softening. "I'm not saying that, Gavin," he said gently. "What I'm saying is, what you were doing was antithetical to your soul. So, to cope, you create fantasies around it to make it more palatable. It's not unusual to recreate fantasies throughout your life because of it."

Gavin's eyes narrowed, his voice lowering. "…like Colton?" he asked, his mind whirling.

Dr. Jacobs placed his hand on top of Gavin's, his voice quiet but firm. "Please, Gavin," he said softly. "Let me help you get through this. Let me help you understand it… and let go of it. What you have with Eric is real. It's good. It's worth fighting for."

Gavin sat there, feeling like the room had shrunk in on him. His chest felt tight, his breath coming in short bursts as he wrestled with the emotions surging through him. Slowly, he stood up, shaking his head. "This was a complete mistake," he said, his voice cold. "I should have never come back. I'm seriously fine. I don't need help."

Dr. Jacobs sat up straighter, his eyes filled with concern. "Gavin, don't be like this," he urged, but there was an edge of exasperation to his voice now.

Gavin walked toward the door, his hand gripping the handle. "It's fine," he said, his voice clipped. "I have everything completely under control."

"I don't believe that, Gavin," Dr. Jacobs said, standing up now, his voice carrying a note of urgency. "Please! Don't walk out this way."

Gavin paused, his hand still on the doorknob, but he didn't turn around. "Believe what you want," he muttered, his voice flat. "I'm leaving."

And with that, Gavin walked out of the office, the door clicking softly shut behind him, leaving Dr. Jacobs standing in the middle of the room, staring after him.

Chapter 21

Gavin's frustration simmered as he stormed down the street, the echo of his last conversation with Dr. Jacobs playing on a loop in his head. How could Dr. Jacobs even suggest that Colton wasn't real, that their relationship was some kind of fantasy Gavin had created to escape reality?

It was absurd.

The memory of Colton's art gallery painting—the one of Gavin, naked and vulnerable—flashed in his mind. Colton had seen him and understood him in a way no one else did. That painting proved it.

He couldn't let Dr. Jacobs' ridiculous insinuations go. Maybe he should pay Colton a visit and remind himself of how real their connection was. The thought gave him a twisted sense of satisfaction, and before he realized it, Gavin had pulled out his phone and searched for Colton's name online. It wasn't hard to find information on him—Colton had always been good at self-promotion. Gavin's eyes landed on an upcoming open gallery showing tonight, one Colton hadn't invited him to.

Perfect.

Without thinking twice, Gavin hailed a cab and made his way across the city. The gallery was in a trendy district, surrounded by upscale bars and boutiques, the kind of place that Colton thrived in. Gavin stepped out of the cab and into the cool evening air, adjusting his coat as he strode toward the entrance. The gallery's large glass windows showed the brightly lit space inside. Art enthusiasts milled about, drinks in hand, admiring the various pieces on display.

As he entered, Gavin made a beeline for the bar, feeling the need for a drink to steady his nerves. The bartender—a stylish young woman with short, dark hair—smiled as he approached.

"What can I get you?" she asked, her voice friendly but professional.

"A dirty martini, please... with vodka," Gavin replied, leaning against the counter as he scanned the room. It seemed to be his usual drink here at the gallery now.

The bartender nodded, skillfully preparing the cocktail. Gavin's eyes swept across the gallery, searching for Colton. The crowd was filled with well-dressed patrons, their conversations blending into a low whisper beneath the ambient music playing softly in the background. When the drink arrived, Gavin took a long sip, savoring the sharp taste of vodka and olive brine. He was ready to surprise Colton—ready to remind him just how real their connection was.

But then he saw it.

Across the gallery, near a collection of abstract paintings, Colton stood with his hand resting on the lower back of another man. Gavin's stomach dropped as he watched them, the intimacy of the gesture undeniable. The man—slightly shorter, with tousled brown hair and an artist's effortless charm—laughed at something Colton said, leaning into him ever so slightly.

Gavin's grip tightened around his glass, his breath catching in his throat. He was about to march over when a voice interrupted his thoughts.

"Hey, you alright?"

Gavin turned to find another man standing beside him, clearly having noticed his reaction. He was well-dressed, with sharp features and an air of confidence, but his eyes held a certain curiosity.

Gavin forced a smile, though it didn't reach his eyes. "Yeah," he replied, though his voice was tight. "Just... wondering who that guy with Colton Anderson is."

The man raised an eyebrow, following Gavin's gaze. "Oh, that's Jake Langland," he explained casually. "He's an artist, like Colton. They've collaborated on a few pieces together. Some of the paintings are pretty... *suggestive,* if you know what I mean."

Gavin felt his chest tighten further, the knot of jealousy twisting inside him. He turned back to his drink, downing it quickly as the man continued talking.

"Yeah, they seem close," the man added, oblivious to Gavin's discomfort. "*Really* close."

Before Gavin could respond, Colton's eyes suddenly locked onto his from across the room. The playful smirk on Colton's face faltered, his hand slipping from Jake's back as he straightened up. Gavin turned on his heel, setting his glass down with more force than necessary, and made a beeline for the exit. The gallery felt too small, too claustrophobic, the walls closing in on him with every step.

But as he burst out into the cool night air, Colton was already behind him.

"Gavin, wait!" Colton's voice rang out, catching up to him just as Gavin reached the narrow alley beside the gallery.

Gavin stopped, his hands clenched into fists as he whirled around to face Colton.

"What the hell was that?" Gavin spat, his voice harsh with accusation.

Colton raised his hands in defense, his expression softening. "It's not what you think."

"Really?" Gavin crossed his arms, his eyes narrowing. "Because it sure looked like you were pretty cozy with your *collaborator*."

Colton sighed, running a hand through his hair. "Jake is just a friend. A collaborator, like you said. Nothing more."

Gavin wasn't convinced. "I don't believe you," he snapped, turning on his heel to storm off again. But Colton grabbed his arm, stopping him.

"I'm not having sex with him," Colton said, his voice low but sincere.

Gavin pulled his arm free, glaring at him. "I didn't ask that," he shot back. "I simply asked who he was. That's a perfectly reasonable question."

Colton sighed, his agitation evident. "Oh, come on, Gavin. It was the way you asked it. I could read between the lines."

Gavin shook his head, anger bubbling to the surface. "You know," he began, his voice trembling with emotion. "You showed me that painting you made of me, and I thought I meant something special to you. But I'm out of the picture for a few days, and true to form, you've already moved on to someone else."

Colton stepped closer, his eyes pleading. "I haven't moved on," he insisted. "You mean something to me, Gavin. You know that."

Gavin scoffed, but before he could say another word, Colton grabbed him by the shoulders, pushing him gently back against the brick wall of the alley. The sudden movement sent a jolt through Gavin's body, and before he could react, Colton's lips were on his, urgent and demanding.

They shoved each other, the tension between them exploding into something physical and raw. Gavin's back hit the wall, the rough texture scraping against his coat as Colton kissed him harder. Their hands groped and pulled, desperate to be closer. The world outside the alley faded away; the only sounds were their ragged breathing and the faint thrum of the city beyond.

Gavin pulled back, his lips swollen and breathless. "What are we doing?" he whispered, his voice filled with confusion and desire.

Colton smirked, his hands still gripping Gavin's waist. "This," he stated before kissing him again, deeper this time.

They continued to kiss, their bodies pressed tight against each other, the weight of their arguments dissolving into the passion that had always been there, simmering just beneath the surface.

As they kissed, Colton's hands began to explore Gavin's body. He ran his fingers through Gavin's hair before moving them down to his ass, giving it a firm squeeze.

Gavin moaned softly into the kiss, his hands finding their way to the waistband of Colton's jeans. He fumbled with the button and zipper, eager to get Colton's pants off.

Colton chuckled against Gavin's lips. "Not so fast, babe. I've got other plans for you."

Gavin raised an eyebrow in curiosity. "Oh really? And what might those plans be?"

"You'll see soon enough." Colton winked at Gavin before grabbing him by the waist and lifting him up. Gavin let out a surprised gasp as he found himself airborne, his legs instinctively wrapping around Colton's waist.

Colton carried Gavin over to the brick wall, pressing him against it before releasing him. With one hand, he tugged Gavin's jeans down to his ankles, leaving him completely exposed and vulnerable.

Gavin shivered in anticipation, his breath coming out in short, sharp gasps. "Colton, please…"

"Shh, just relax and enjoy it," Colton whispered seductively into Gavin's ear before nipping at the sensitive lobe.

Colton reached between them, his fingers tracing a path down Gavin's chest and stomach until they finally reached their destination. He gave Gavin's throbbing cock a firm squeeze, eliciting a loud moan.

Gavin writhed against the brick wall, his hips bucking involuntarily as Colton continued to tease and torment his aching cock.

"You like that, don't you?" Colton asked, his voice thick with desire.

"Yes," Gavin panted, his voice barely above a whisper.

Colton smirked at Gavin's response before leaning down

and taking the head of Gavin's dick into his mouth. He sucked on it greedily, his tongue swirling around the sensitive tip.

Gavin threw his head back against the wall, his eyes squeezed shut as he tried to stifle the sounds of pleasure that threatened to escape his lips.

Suddenly, Colton pulled back, leaving Gavin's cock wet and throbbing. He grinned up at Gavin, his eyes sparkling with mischief.

"You want me inside you, don't you?" Colton asked, his voice low and husky.

Gavin nodded eagerly, his cheeks flushed with desire. "Yes, please…"

Colton didn't waste any more time. With a sly grin, he spit on his fingers and began to massage Gavin's hole with his wet fingers. He started off by gently circling around the entrance before finally pushing one finger inside.

Gavin gasped at the sudden intrusion, his body tensing up suddenly before relaxing once again. Colton continued to work his finger in and out of Gavin's hole, gradually stretching it out and preparing it for what was to come.

After a few minutes of this, Colton added a second finger, causing Gavin to cry out in both pleasure and pain.

"You okay?" Colton asked, his voice filled with concern.

"Yes," Gavin managed to choke out between gasps. "I-it just feels so intense…"

"Good, because I'm about to make you feel even better." With that, Colton placed his hands under Gavin's ass and hoisted him into the air again against the brick wall. He quickly inserted the head of his cock inside Gavin.

Gavin let out a loud cry of pleasure as Colton pushed himself deeper inside him. The sensation of having Colton's thick shaft filling him up to the brim without lube was almost too much for him to handle.

Colton held Gavin's legs steady in the air as he began to thrust in and out of him, his hips moving in a smooth, steady rhythm.

"Fuck, Gavin... you feel so fucking good," Colton groaned, his breath coming out in short, sharp gasps.

Gavin moaned loudly in response, his entire body trembling with pleasure. "Harder... fucking harder!" he begged, his voice filled with desperation.

Colton didn't need any more encouragement. He increased the pace and force of his thrusts, pounding mercilessly into Gavin's hole.

Gavin screamed out in ecstasy, his voice echoing off the walls of the alleyway. "Oh God, yes! Right there, Colton, right fucking there!"

Colton grinned at Gavin, his eyes filled with a fierce sense of satisfaction. "That's it, just let go and enjoy it," he teased as he continued to fuck him hard and fast against the brick wall.

The intensity of the moment was almost too much for Gavin to handle. He could feel his orgasm building up inside him, threatening to spill over.

"Oh fuck, Colton, I'm gonna cum!" Gavin cried out, his voice filled with both pleasure and pain.

"Do it, babe. Fucking cum for me," Colton commanded, his voice thick with desire.

With a loud cry of pleasure, Gavin finally tipped over the edge, his cock pulsing wildly as he shot out thick, creamy ropes of cum all over Colton's chest and stomach.

Seeing Gavin reach his climax sent Colton over the edge as well. With a loud grunt of pleasure, he thrust himself as deep inside Gavin's hole as far as he possibly could before finally filling him up completely with his own hot, sticky load.

For a few seconds, neither of them moved or spoke as they both struggled to catch their breath. Finally, Colton carefully lowered Gavin back down onto the ground before tucking himself back into his pants.

Gavin stood in the alleyway, his face flushed with pleasure

and exhaustion. He looked at Colton with a satisfied smile.

"So, was skipping foreplay worth it?" Gavin asked, his voice filled with a sense of smug satisfaction.

Colton chuckled softly before leaning down and giving Gavin a deep, passionate kiss. "Definitely," he murmured seductively into Gavin's ear as they both stood there in the alleyway, their bodies still slick with sweat and cum. "Definitely."

Chapter 22

The day had been a whirlwind, but Gavin was riding the high of another successful real estate sale. The sun poured through the large windows of the property he had just shown to his client, casting a warm glow over the sleek, modern interior. Everything had gone smoothly—the client was thrilled with the space, a sprawling penthouse overlooking the river with floor-to-ceiling windows, a state-of-the-art kitchen, and a private rooftop terrace. It was the kind of place Gavin himself could see calling home if things had been different.

Gavin led the client through the final walkthrough, the energy between them easy and confident.

"This place is exactly what I was looking for," the client said, their voice filled with excitement as they ran their hand along the marble countertop in the kitchen. "It's perfect. You really nailed it, Gavin."

"I'm glad you think so," Gavin replied with a grin. "I knew the second we walked in that this was the one for you."

They continued to discuss the finer details of the sale—closing dates and any last-minute negotiations with the seller. The whole process was seamless, and Gavin felt that familiar rush of satisfaction that came with closing another deal. When everything was set, they shook hands, sealing the transaction.

"Looking forward to seeing you at the final signing," Gavin said, smiling as his client left the penthouse.

With the deal wrapped up, Gavin headed back to his office. The adrenaline of the sale began to fade, leaving him feeling the weight of his personal life once more. As he sat at his desk, his phone buzzed, and for a brief moment, Gavin felt a glimmer of hope that it might be Eric, or even Ashton, sending a message. But when he glanced at the screen, it was Colton calling.

A strange mix of emotions washed over him as he picked up the phone.

"Hey," Gavin said, trying to keep his voice steady.

Colton's tone on the other end wasn't as upbeat as usual. "Hey, Gav. Listen, I'm really sorry, but I've got to cancel tonight. Something came up, and I won't be able to make it."

Gavin blinked, caught off guard by the sudden cancellation. The sting of disappointment hit him quickly, but he masked it with a chuckle. "Oh," he said, trying to sound casual. "Well, I was actually going to cancel on you, too. I've been thinking… I really need to work on my marriage."

There was a pause on the line, and Gavin felt his chest tighten as he waited for Colton's response.

"I see," Colton finally said, his voice quieter now. "Well, I guess that works out, then."

"Yeah… I guess so," Gavin said, forcing a smile even though Colton couldn't see him. "I mean, it's just—Eric and Ashton mean the world to me, you know? I need to get things right with them."

"Of course," Colton replied, his tone still distant.

The conversation quickly ended, and Gavin hung up, feeling hollow. He sat there in silence, staring at his phone. He had told Colton he wanted to work on his marriage, but the words hadn't felt entirely true. His mind was already swirling with guilt. Had he just sabotaged something important? The thought gnawed at him.

A few minutes later, the guilt became too much. Gavin grabbed his phone again, scrolling through his recent calls, and tapped Colton's number. He couldn't just leave things like that.

The phone rang several times before someone picked up, but it wasn't Colton.

"Hello?" a man's voice answered, casual and unfamiliar.

Gavin blinked, slightly thrown. "Uh, sorry, is this Colton's phone?"

"Yeah," the voice replied. "Are you looking for Colton?"

Gavin felt a sinking feeling in his stomach. "Yes," he said slowly. "Who is this?"

"It's Jake," the man replied smoothly.

The name hit Gavin like a punch to the gut. *Jake*. The same Jake he'd seen with Colton at the gallery, the same man who had been all over him.

"Oh... um," Gavin stammered, trying to process what was happening. "Well, um... where's Colton?"

Jake's voice remained calm, almost indifferent. "He's in the shower. Can I give him a message?"

Gavin's heart was pounding now, the jealousy and fury swirling in his chest. He hung up without saying another word, his hands shaking as he tossed the phone onto his desk. His mind raced, replaying the events of the gallery and now, *this*.

Gavin stood up, pacing the length of his office, the walls suddenly feeling too close. The betrayal burned through him, the feeling that, once again, he had been cast aside, replaced. How could Colton claim Gavin meant something to him when another man was in his apartment?

Anger welled up inside him, but underneath it all, a deep sadness weighed on him. He had lied to Colton, saying he wanted to fix things with Eric, but the truth was, he had wanted to believe that Colton still cared, that their connection was more than just fleeting.

Now, that hope seemed to be slipping through his fingers.

The sharp click of Gavin's shoes echoed through the hallway as he stormed toward Colton's apartment, the rage boiling inside him. He could still hear Jake's calm and casual voice in his head, telling him Colton was in the shower. The mere thought of it made Gavin's blood burn hotter. He had tried to move past it and rationalize Colton's actions, but this—this was the final straw.

When he reached Colton's door, Gavin didn't hesitate. His knuckles rapped hard against the wood, the force behind each knock reflecting the storm raging within him. Shortly, the door swung open, and there stood Colton, shirtless, his bare chest still glistening from what was clearly a recent shower. He was in the middle of pulling a T-shirt over his head when he looked up at Gavin, his expression one of surprise, mixed with something almost like guilt.

"I wanted to see you one last time," Gavin spat, pushing past him and barging into the apartment, his eyes scanning the room with disgust.

"What are you talking about?" Colton asked, his voice confused, though there was an edge to it that didn't sit right with Gavin.

The apartment looked normal for the most part—comfortable, almost too comfortable for Gavin's liking. Canvases were leaning against the walls, paintbrushes strewn across a table, and the faint scent of fresh paint lingered in the air. But it wasn't the artistic disarray that bothered Gavin. It was the faint signs of something else—two wine glasses sitting by the bed, half-filled with red wine, a bottle of lube carelessly placed on the nightstand.

"I should've known," Gavin sneered, turning to face Colton, who was now standing awkwardly by the door, his hands halfway to his sides as if unsure of what to do. "I should always know you're amazing at lying, but I keep falling for it somehow."

Colton frowned, his brow furrowed in confusion. "What are you talking about?"

"Where is he?" Gavin's voice cut through the air like a blade, sharp and cold.

"Where is who?" Colton asked, his tone rising with confusion.

Gavin turned, his fists clenched at his sides. "Jake. I called your cell phone, and *he* picked it up while you were in the shower. I wanted to call you back—to tell you how hard this was for me. I was actually feeling guilty for letting you go. I opened my heart to you—and you did it again! You fucked me over!"

Without warning, Gavin shoved Colton hard in the chest, his body reacting to the wave of betrayal and fury washing over him. Colton stumbled back slightly, caught off guard by the sudden aggression.

"Gavin, stop!" Colton protested, his hands raising defensively, but Gavin was already moving toward the nightstand.

His eyes landed on the wine glasses and the bottle of lube, and he felt another surge of anger pulse through him. He pointed at the setup, his voice dripping with venom. "And what the hell is that about?" Gavin's voice rose, his eyes flashing. "And don't give me some pathetic excuse about drinking from two glasses. Do us both a favor and don't make me look like a fucking fool because I won't fall for it again!"

He shoved Colton again, harder this time, his heart pounding in his chest.

Colton's frustration was clear now, his face flushing as he grabbed Gavin's arm to steady him. "Hey! Listen to me!" Colton shouted, his voice firm but desperate. "Jake means nothing to me! He's just crashing here for a few days. That's all. I swear to you. So just relax, sit down, and I'll grab you a drink."

But Gavin was beyond calming down. He could hear Colton's words, but they felt hollow, like an echo of excuses he had heard before. Colton turned and headed into the kitchen, but Gavin's eyes remained fixed on the two wine glasses by the bed, the reminder of what he was sure had happened here.

His mind raced, his thoughts spinning out of control. He wanted Colton to pay for this—wanted him to feel the same sting of betrayal Gavin had felt. Without thinking, he reached for the half-empty bottle of wine on the nightstand, the deep red liquid swirling inside.

As Colton moved farther into the kitchen, his back turned, Gavin acted. In one swift motion, he lifted the bottle and splashed its contents across the canvases propped against the wall. The wine splattered across Colton's latest works, the vibrant reds and purples streaking down the carefully painted surfaces, ruining hours of labor in seconds.

The sound of liquid hitting the canvas was loud in the silence of the room, and Colton spun around just as Gavin was already heading toward the door.

"Where are you going?" Colton demanded, his voice laced with shock and fury.

Gavin didn't even turn around. His voice was cold, the finality clear in his words. "Go to hell!" he snapped before storming out of the apartment and slamming the door behind him.

Outside, the cool night air hit his face, but it did nothing to cool the fire burning inside him. He had thought confronting Colton would bring him some sense of satisfaction, some closure. But instead, he felt hollow, as if the argument had only opened up more wounds.

As Gavin walked away from the building, his heart pounded in his chest, the sting of betrayal and rage still fresh.

Chapter 23

Colton's heart raced as he stood in his apartment, staring at the mess Gavin had made. The red wine dripped from his paintings, streaking down the canvases like the blood of his hard work bleeding out before his eyes. The vibrant colors he had painstakingly mixed and layered were now ruined, the deep burgundy of the wine seeping into the fabric, warping the lines and distorting the images. Anger boiled inside him, a furious heat rising in his chest.

Without a second thought, Colton grabbed his jacket from the back of the chair, threw it on, and slipped into his shoes. His jaw clenched, his mind spinning. He couldn't just let Gavin walk out after this—after destroying what meant the most to him. With a single motion, he swung the door open and rushed out, chasing after Gavin.

The cool evening air hit his face as he stepped out of the building, but it did nothing to calm the fire raging inside him. Gavin's silhouette was already disappearing down the street, moving quickly, his steps purposeful. Colton followed at a distance, his shoes hitting the pavement with sharp, angry taps, the noise swallowed by the clamor of the city around him.

The streets were quieter now, the hustle of earlier evening hours fading into the stillness of night. Streetlights cast long shadows over the buildings, and the occasional sound of a car passing by filled the air. Colton kept his distance, his eyes locked on Gavin as he wound through the familiar streets and turned onto a quieter road lined with apartment buildings.

Colton's breath came in short, controlled bursts as he followed him, his fists still clenched. He wanted to scream, to demand answers, but something in him held back, kept him creeping behind, waiting for the right time. Gavin walked with a determination that made Colton's chest tighten. *Where was he going? Was he meeting someone?* Or was this just Gavin trying to get away from what he had done?

After several blocks, Gavin finally slowed his pace, turning toward an old brick apartment building with ivy climbing its walls. The building had weathered stone steps leading up to the entrance. Colton narrowed his eyes as Gavin opened the front door and slipped inside without hesitation. He followed, quickening his pace, slipping into the building just before the door fully closed and locked behind Gavin.

The lobby was dimly lit, with faded wallpaper and a worn-out staircase leading upward. Colton watched as Gavin climbed two flights of stairs, his footfalls echoing in the empty space. At the top of the stairs, Gavin turned toward a door marked "D." Without missing a beat, he unlocked it and stepped inside, disappearing into the apartment.

Colton wasn't far behind.

Before the door could even close, Colton burst through it, slamming it back open as he stormed inside.

"Are you insane!? Are you out of your fucking mind!?" Colton's voice echoed off the walls as he stepped into the small, modest apartment, his face flushed with anger. The door swung shut behind him with a loud click, leaving the two of them alone in the narrow hallway.

Gavin spun around, his eyes wide with surprise, clearly not expecting Colton to have followed him all the way here. He opened his mouth to speak, but Colton was already advancing toward him, fury pouring out with every word.

"Do you have any idea how long I spent on those paintings!?" Colton shouted, his voice rising with each sentence. "Do you have any clue how much they would've gone for? And forget the money—they meant something to me!"

Gavin stood still, his expression unreadable, as Colton

continued his tirade.

"And just for the record, not that it's any of your business—I'm *not* sleeping with Jake." Colton's voice was sharp, almost bitter, as if the accusation itself had wounded him more than Gavin's actions.

Gavin scoffed, rolling his eyes as he crossed his arms over his chest. "Oh, stop it already!" he snapped back. "I'm not a fucking idiot, Colton."

Colton's eyes narrowed, his jaw tightening as he took a step closer. "And neither am I," he growled. "Jake has a boyfriend back home. He's working on a house renovation. He's just staying with me temporarily until the place is ready."

Colton stood in the middle of the small apartment, his eyes narrowing as he surveyed the space. The walls were pretty bare, and there was sparse furniture. Something was off about it all, something that didn't sit right. The longer he stood there, the more out of place everything felt.

Colton turned slowly, his gaze falling on a fireplace mantle that held a single photo frame. Walking over, he lifted the frame, staring at the image of a little boy who looked like the spitting image of Gavin. The resemblance was uncanny.

"This is you, isn't it?" Colton asked, a strange curiosity lacing his words as he turned to Gavin, holding the picture up.

Gavin's face tightened, his movements quick and sharp as he stormed over, snatching the photo from Colton's hand. "Get out, now!" Gavin demanded, his voice full of warning.

But Colton didn't budge. Instead, he stared at Gavin, his mind racing as realization began to sink in. His lips parted slightly, his expression a mix of confusion and something darker. "This is your place, isn't it?" he said, his voice quieter now, almost as if the revelation was too big to process all at once.

Gavin didn't respond. His face was hard as stone. He turned his back on Colton, heading toward the door to lead him out, but Colton wasn't done. He went down the hall, his footsteps quickening, and made his way to a bedroom. Gavin's voice rang out behind him, growing more frantic.

"I said get the hell out of here!" Gavin's words carried a desperate edge, but Colton wasn't listening anymore.

Colton entered the bedroom, his eyes scanning the space. It seemed cold in its lack of personal touches. The bed was neatly made, but the room felt empty—empty in a way that suggested it wasn't truly lived in by two people. There were no signs of another soul, no shared life. Colton walked over to the closet and pulled open the door, revealing only one set of clothes—no extra jackets, no additional shoes.

"You live here alone, don't you?" Colton asked, his voice calm yet laced with the sting of truth. "There's no husband. No kid… is there? You made it all up, didn't you?"

Gavin stood in the doorway, staring at him blankly, his eyes devoid of the sharp fire they had held just seconds ago. He looked almost defeated, his shoulders slumped as if he had finally been caught in a lie too big to escape.

Colton's gaze drifted over to the nightstand, and that's when he saw it. A photo of Eric, Ashton, and Gavin, perfectly placed—except something wasn't right. Gavin's face didn't quite fit. It was clearly a cutout that was taped to the image. Colton stepped closer, his hand shaking slightly as he reached for the photo. Slowly, he peeled back the tape with Gavin's face on it, revealing the original face beneath Gavin's.

The man in the picture wasn't Gavin. It was someone else entirely—a man with a kind face. Colton's heart pounded as he stared at the picture, the pieces falling into place with horrifying clarity.

"This guy… I've seen him before," Colton muttered, his voice thick with disbelief. "Wait a minute… He's the guy from the news. That music teacher at the elementary school. The one who fell off the cliff, isn't he?"

Gavin didn't move, didn't flinch. He just stood there, watching Colton with a hollow gaze.

Colton dropped the photo back onto the nightstand, his chest tightening as the weight of the truth pressed down on him. This was bigger than jealousy, bigger than whatever affair they'd been having. This was a lie so twisted, so dark, that he could barely breathe through the shock of it all.

"What the hell, Gavin?" Colton's voice trembled slightly. He stepped back, distancing himself from the man he thought he knew.

Gavin's face remained blank, but his silence said more than any explanation ever could.

Colton stared at Gavin, disbelief and horror etched on his face as he took another step back. The photo of the music teacher was still burned into his mind. The room seemed to close in around them, the air heavy with the weight of unspoken truths and the tension that crackled between them.

"You're out of your mind, aren't you, Gavin?" Colton's voice was low, almost a whisper, as if he were speaking to a stranger, someone he no longer recognized.

Gavin's eyes darkened, his face tight with barely contained rage. His voice was cold and deliberate as he hissed, "Get... out... of my life."

Colton's jaw clenched, his face a mixture of anger and disgust. "Believe me, I'm going..." He turned to leave, but something made him pause before he did. He glanced back at Gavin, his eyes filled with a disturbing clarity. "Who is that other man in the picture? Does he even exist?"

Gavin's voice was sharp and defensive. "Of course he does."

Colton shook his head, incredulous. "Well, someone better warn him about you." His words were laced with venom as he spun on his heel, heading for the door.

Gavin stood there, frozen, his mind racing. This was all falling apart too quickly. He couldn't let Colton walk out, couldn't let him ruin everything. Panic set in. His heart pounded in his chest as he watched Colton heading toward the door, each step a hammer to Gavin's already fragile sense of control.

Without thinking, he darted toward the kitchen, his hands trembling as he grabbed a knife from the wooden knife block on the counter. His breath came in short, frantic gasps as he tucked the knife into his back pocket, his mind racing for a solution. He couldn't let this spiral out of control—not now, not like this.

"Wait! Colton!" Gavin called out, his voice shaky, his steps hurried as he chased after him.

Colton stopped suddenly, turning around with an exasperated look on his face. He was tired of the drama, tired of Gavin's instability. But before he could say anything, Gavin was already standing in front of him, his eyes wild with desperation.

"Please," Gavin begged, his voice breaking. "Don't do this. Don't ruin my family."

Colton's face softened for a moment, but only briefly. He grabbed Gavin by the shoulders, his grip firm but not cruel. "That's not your family, Gavin," Colton said sternly, his voice calm but urgent. "Seriously, you're being insane. Let me get you professional help."

Tears welled up in Gavin's eyes, his heart shattering with every word. "No! Please don't! Please don't destroy my family. It's all I have!" His voice was a desperate wail, the sobs catching in his throat as he clung to the only thing he thought he could hold onto—his delusion.

Colton's grip tightened as he shook Gavin gently. "This is out of hand! You need help! You're going to hurt somebody!"

"I don't want to hurt anybody!" Gavin screamed, his voice raw and full of agony. But his hand moved before his mind could stop him. The knife was out of his pocket and in his hand, the blade flashing in the dim light of the apartment.

In a swift, instinctive motion, Gavin plunged the knife into Colton's side.

Colton gasped, his eyes wide with shock as he stumbled forward, his hands clutching at his stomach, where blood was already beginning to seep through his shirt. His body convulsed in pain as he looked at Gavin, his face twisted in disbelief.

Gavin pulled the knife out, his hand shaking violently as he looked down at the blood now staining his fingers. But he wasn't done. In another frantic motion, he drove the knife in again, the blade sinking into Colton's body for the second time.

Colton yelped, his body collapsing into Gavin's arms, his weight heavy and warm. His breath came in shallow gasps, his hands weakly trying to push Gavin away, but there was no strength left.

Gavin held him as he sank to the floor, tears streaming down his face as he whispered, "I'm so sorry, Colton. I'm so sorry... I can't let you hurt me... I can't let you hurt my family and what we have..."

Colton's body went limp in his arms, the last bit of life draining from him as he slumped to the ground. His blood pooled around them, warm and sticky on the cold floor, staining Gavin's clothes and hands. The apartment was silent, save for Gavin's soft, broken sobs.

He let the knife slip from his fingers, the metallic clatter echoing in the stillness. Gavin sat there, his hands covered in Colton's blood, his mind a chaotic mess of regret and fear. He hadn't meant to kill him. He just wanted to stop him. Just wanted to keep everything from falling apart.

But now it was too late.

Gavin looked down at Colton's lifeless body, the reality of what he had done crashing down on him. He had to get rid of it. The body, the evidence—everything. He couldn't let this ruin everything he had worked so hard to protect.

He stood up, his legs shaky and weak as he stared at the bloodied scene before him. His mind raced with possibilities, with what he had to do next. He couldn't afford to lose his family. Not now. Not ever.

This was just another mess he had to clean up. He would do whatever it took to keep his world intact, no matter how far he had to go.

Chapter 24

The lake house was stunning, perched on the serene edge of a shimmering body of water, its expansive windows capturing the glint of sunlight reflecting off the surface. Gavin and his client strolled through the grand entryway, which opened into a spacious living room with vaulted ceilings and exposed wooden beams. The walls were painted a calming sage, complementing the natural beauty of the landscape outside. The smell of fresh wood and the faint aroma of lake air gave the house a warm, inviting feel.

"This place is incredible," the client marveled, running her hand along the edge of the pure white quartz kitchen island. The kitchen itself was a work of art—custom cabinetry in soft gray tones, and brass fixtures that added a touch of elegance. The kitchen opened to a large dining area, perfect for entertaining guests with views that stretched out to the water.

"It really is," Gavin agreed, smiling as he gestured toward the floor-to-ceiling windows that lined the back wall of the living room. "The views, the design—it's like something out of a dream."

The client moved toward the kitchen, taking in the open-plan layout that flowed effortlessly into the living space. "I can see us hosting dinners here," she said, her voice filled with excitement. "Maybe put some custom seating in this corner... definitely a larger dining table." She waved her hand, gesturing toward the vast, sunlit area. "It's just beautiful."

Gavin nodded, envisioning it all with her. The house had a richness to it, the kind of place that made people feel like they'd found their forever home. It was no surprise the client was so taken with it.

They wandered deeper into the house, through the hallway that led to the bedrooms, each one tastefully decorated with soft neutrals and large windows that offered a glimpse of the trees and the lake just beyond. Gavin paused as the client picked up a framed photo from a side table in the master bedroom.

The picture showed two men, arms wrapped around each other, standing on the front porch of the lake house. Between them stood a young boy, grinning brightly at the camera. The little family looked radiant, full of joy. The client studied the image briefly, her brow furrowing with curiosity.

"Beautiful family," the client said, turning to Gavin. "What do they do?"

Gavin hesitated. He knew that image well. He could see Eric's familiar smile in the picture, his strong arm draped protectively around Jason. And there, in the center, was Ashton, looking as happy as ever. It was surreal seeing their life frozen in a frame like this, knowing all too well the real story behind it.

"I really shouldn't say," Gavin replied after a pause, his voice soft. "But one of them is a doctor, and the other is a music teacher."

The client nodded, eyes still lingering on the photo. "A doctor and a music teacher... That's lovely. I wonder why they aren't staying here. This place is magnificent. I imagine it must have been a tough decision to sell it."

Gavin swallowed, his heart tightening slightly at the truth he was holding back. He knew why they weren't staying here. He knew all about the unraveling of their relationship, the lies, and the heartbreak.

"From what I gathered," Gavin said carefully, "they're no longer together."

The client looked surprised, tilting her head as she set the photo back down. "What a shame. They look so perfect."

"Yeah," Gavin murmured, glancing out the window to

the lake beyond. "I'm sure it was at one time. But maybe some things just aren't meant to last forever."

The client sighed, nodding in agreement. "I suppose you're right. Well, we've seen enough. My husband and I have discussed it, and we want to buy it. No need for negotiations. The asking price is more than fair, and we don't want anyone else swooping in and taking it from us."

Gavin felt a rush of relief. "That's wonderful news," he said with a bright smile. "This house really suits you perfectly. I'll head back to the office, draw up the offer, and get in touch with the selling agent, who I know very well. We'll make it official."

The client beamed, walking back toward the main living area and taking one last look around. "Thank you, Gavin. You really found us our dream home."

"Of course," Gavin replied, the warmth of the sale settling into him. "I'll be in touch soon."

As they left the house and made their way back to the driveway, Gavin's thoughts returned to the picture of Eric, Jason, and Ashton. A perfect family, now fractured beyond repair. He pushed the thought aside, focusing on the task at hand. Another sale, another chapter closed.

But no matter how many sales he made, there was always a piece of him that lingered in the past, tied to the people and memories that had once filled these houses.

Gavin walked into the real estate office with a spring in his step, his smile wide and confident. The usual office chatter filled the air, but his focus was solely on the triumph of his latest sale. The lake house—*Spencer's* lake house, in which Spencer was the selling agent—was off the market and not a moment too soon. He couldn't wait to share the news.

As he made his way to Spencer's office, the scent of freshly brewed coffee and the muted sound of typing floated through the air. Spencer was hunched over his computer, fingers flying across the keyboard, completely engrossed. But the minute he caught sight of Gavin standing in the doorway, his smile widening, Spencer's face lit up with recognition.

"I know that beautiful white smile," Spencer said, leaning back in his chair with a grin. "I see it whenever you've made an amazing sale. Let me guess, was this one my lake house deal?"

Gavin nodded, and Spencer, unable to contain his excitement, leaped from his chair and punched the air in celebration. "Hell yes!" he shouted, his enthusiasm infectious. "How much?"

"They want to give the full asking price," Gavin said, his voice calm but tinged with pride. "No negotiations."

Spencer practically tackled Gavin in a hug, his excitement palpable. "That's amazing, man! Holy shit. You are seriously the best!" Spencer clapped Gavin on the shoulder before stepping back, pacing the room with exhilaration. "I knew you had this in the bag, but full asking price? You're a legend!"

Gavin smirked, pleased with how smoothly the transaction had gone. He felt the surge of adrenaline that always came after a successful deal, and it never got old.

As Gavin was about to head out, Spencer paused, a thoughtful look crossing his face. "Actually, I have an idea." He sat back down, leaning forward, his eyes gleaming with excitement. "You're the one who did all the work and made this magic happen. Why don't you be the one to present the offer to my client?"

Gavin blinked, slightly taken aback. "Really? You want me to do that?"

Spencer nodded firmly, his grin unwavering. "Of course! You deserve it. I'll let him know you'll be stopping by later tonight. His name's Eric Clarke. He's a doctor, great guy... but he's had one hell of a year."

Gavin's stomach twisted at the mention of Eric's name, though he kept his expression neutral, masking the immediate dread rising within him. "Oh? What happened?" he asked, feigning interest and curiosity, though he already knew far too well.

Spencer sighed, leaning back in his chair as he rubbed the back of his neck. "His husband died in a terrible accident. Fell off a cliff, apparently. Lost his footing while hiking down the trail. A real tragedy."

Gavin felt a twinge of something—guilt, perhaps, or maybe something darker—deep in his chest, but he kept his face blank, nodding slowly as he processed the news.

"My God! That's... that's awful," Gavin said, injecting his voice with just the right amount of shock and sympathy.

"Yeah, it's really terrible. They've got an eight-year-old son, too. Poor kid's been through a lot. That's why Eric's selling the house. He wants to move closer to the hospital and make the commute easier so he can be home more with his son as much as possible after everything."

Gavin felt his heart pound at the mention of Ashton, the little boy he had once known so well, and of Eric—*his* Eric—trying to rebuild his life after the tragedy. His head swam with memories, memories he at least thought he had, but he kept his focus on the conversation at hand.

"I get it," Gavin said softly, nodding. "That makes sense. Family comes first."

Spencer smiled, clearly pleased with Gavin's response. "Exactly. And I know Eric will be relieved to hear the house is going to someone who will appreciate it as much as his family did."

Gavin shifted slightly, the tension in his chest tightening. "I'll meet him tonight, then," he said. "Go over the offer, get everything signed off."

Spencer clapped his hands together. "Great! I'll let him know you're coming. I'm sure he'll appreciate the personal touch. And hey, don't be a stranger. We need to celebrate this sale properly when it's all done!"

Gavin laughed, giving a casual salute as he left the office, but his smile faded as soon as he was in the hallway. The thought of seeing Eric again—*officially* seeing him, face-to-face, in a situation that forced them to interact—left him feeling uneasy but also hopeful.

Later tonight, he would meet Eric Clarke to close the deal, but in Gavin's mind, he knew this wasn't just about real estate. With this meeting, he had other motives and intentions, wanting to get closer to Eric and Ashton.

Chapter 25

Gavin stood in front of the bathroom mirror, his hands methodically working moisturizer into his skin, moving with a precision that mirrored his mood. The warm lighting in the bathroom highlighted the sharp angles of his face, casting shadows that made his expression even more intense. He paused, staring at his reflection, scrutinizing every inch of his appearance.

Tonight had to be perfect.

The lake house sale was a huge success, and tonight, he would meet Eric Clarke—*the* Eric Clarke. Gavin's mind was racing with thoughts of how the evening would unfold. It would be the first time they would actually speak together. Everything was coming full circle. Ashton might even be there. The thought of seeing the boy brought a strange flutter to Gavin's chest—nostalgia, maybe, or something darker. He quickly shook it off, focusing again on his reflection.

He grabbed his hair gel, applied a small amount, and carefully combed his hair back, ensuring every strand was in place. There could be no slip-ups tonight. Not with Eric. Everything needed to go perfectly. He couldn't let any mistakes ruin this. He was so close to securing not just the deal, but some form of control over the recent chaos that had been his life.

As he leaned in closer to the mirror to check his skin, his phone rang, vibrating against the marble countertop. Gavin's eyes glanced at the screen—*Dr. Jacobs*. The therapist had been relentless lately, constantly trying to reach him. Gavin had ignored the calls and the emails, but maybe it was time to finally deal with it.

Sighing, he picked up the phone. "Hello?"

"Gavin, it's Dr. Jacobs. I'm glad I finally reached you. You haven't been returning my emails or calls."

Gavin kept his eyes locked on his reflection, still combing through his hair. "Sorry. I've been busy."

There was a brief pause on the other end before Dr. Jacobs spoke again, his voice low and cautious. "Gavin, I heard about Colton on the news. His body was found in Cedarfall River. He was stabbed… *murdered*. That was your Colton, wasn't it? A well-known local artist. His work is at the gallery on 34th and Lincoln."

The words seemed to hang in the air, but Gavin's face remained unmoved. He glanced at himself in the mirror, adjusting the collar of his shirt. "Sad, isn't it?"

Dr. Jacobs' voice wavered, clearly unsettled by Gavin's cold tone. "You must be devastated… although you don't sound so devastated."

Gavin's lips curled slightly, the faintest hint of a smile as he stared at himself, adjusting his reflection. "I am… really," he said, the lack of conviction in his voice almost laughable.

"Gavin, have you talked to the police?" Dr. Jacobs asked, his concern seeping through the line.

"Why would I?" Gavin's voice was light, as if they were discussing the weather.

"I think you have something to tell them. Things that might help them solve the crime and discover what really happened to Colton to catch his murderer."

Gavin laughed softly, almost mockingly. "How could I possibly help them? I haven't seen Colton recently. Not in a while."

Dr. Jacobs' voice grew more insistent, a hint of irritation creeping in. "Does it not bother you, Gavin? That the man you were involved with was murdered? That he was stabbed to death and his body dumped in a river?"

Gavin's face tightened slightly as he turned his head, observing himself from a different angle. "I'm not bothered by anything, Dr. Jacobs. That seems to be your fantasy. Colton was actually *real*, not just some figment of my imagination, as you suggested in our last meeting. Frankly, I'm starting to feel a bit harassed by your constant calls."

The silence on the other end was heavy, and Gavin could almost feel Dr. Jacobs' growing concern. The psychologist's voice was softer now, almost pleading. "I'm just concerned about you, Gavin. That's all. That's why I'm calling."

"No, it's not, doctor. You want to somehow involve me in Colton's death, and I'm not going there." Gavin paused, tilting his head as if assessing his reflection anew. "Colton probably got involved with the wrong crowd for the wrong reasons and ended up in a hole he couldn't crawl out of. He had a terrible reputation around town for being a liar and a cheater."

Dr. Jacobs' voice hardened. "Well, I just don't believe that, Gavin."

Gavin turned sharply to face the phone, his expression darkening. "What's that supposed to mean?"

"It means I think you need help, Gavin. I don't believe any of this happened the way you say it did. You need to come and see me."

Gavin sighed, growing tired of the conversation. "I'll consider it. Are you at your office right now?"

"Yes. I'll be here for the next hour or so, but I have other arrangements later. Try to swing by soon if you can. If not, I'd love to see you tomorrow."

Gavin smiled, his voice oddly pleasant. "Perfect. If I can't make it in a little while, I'll call you back tomorrow, and we can schedule an appointment."

Dr. Jacobs sounded relieved. "Thank you, Gavin. I think you're being brave and doing the right thing."

"I think so too, doctor," Gavin said, his voice cold and calculated, the smile still lingering on his lips. He ended the call without another word, tossing the phone onto the counter.

He stared back at his reflection, adjusting his collar one last time. This was just another distraction—another obstacle trying to tear down the life he'd built. But it wouldn't work. Not now. Not ever. Tonight had to be perfect.

Gavin stood in front of his closet, meticulously picking through his wardrobe, scrutinizing each garment for its potential to make the perfect impression. Tonight was important. He needed to look flawless. He needed to present the perfect version of himself to Eric Clarke—*Dr. Eric Clarke*, as he often reminded himself—and Ashton, too. His heart raced at the thought.

He pulled out a fitted charcoal gray suit, its fabric sleek and expensive. The subtle sheen of the material caught the light in just the right way, elegant but not too flashy. Beneath it, he selected a crisp white dress shirt, the collar sharp and folded neatly. A silk tie—deep burgundy with delicate diagonal stripes—would add just the right touch of sophistication. He admired the ensemble before carefully slipping it on. His movements were precise, almost ritualistic.

His shoes were polished to a mirror shine, and the leather was smooth and unblemished. They clicked lightly on the hardwood floor as he paced from his closet to the mirror, straightening his tie and ensuring his cufflinks—a modest but tasteful design—were perfectly in place.

Before leaving, Gavin glanced at the photo on his nightstand the one of Eric, Ashton, and himself. Or rather, the one where he had replaced Jason's face with his own. His fingers traced the edge of the frame, and for a moment, a small, nostalgic smile crossed his face. He had been preparing for this for so long. It was only a matter of time before everything fell into place.

His mind drifted to the recent times he'd seen Eric and Ashton, the stolen instances that felt like glimpses into the life he knew he deserved. He remembered the baseball games, sitting inconspicuously in the bleachers, surrounded by cheering parents. No one gave him a second glance, assuming he was there to support another child on the opposing team. But it wasn't just a game to Gavin. It was a chance to watch Ashton and observe the way the boy moved on the field and the way he beamed when he got a hit. And when he snapped those candid photos of Ashton running the bases, it felt almost... *natural*. As if he were already a part of their world, just waiting for the right time to step in.

Of course, Colton never knew where Gavin really was when he told him he was heading to the beach house. It was a lie, a simple one to cover his tracks. Gavin had no intention of meeting Eric and Ashton at the beach. He hadn't even been to that second home, ever. But Colton wouldn't understand. No one could understand the lengths Gavin would go to in order to claim what was his.

As Gavin walked through his apartment, he paused by the neatly arranged shelf in the corner, where several pristine gift boxes and delicate cards were displayed like trophies. Each card was signed in the same elegant cursive: ***To my incredible husband. Thought you'd like this. Love, Eric.*** A smile tugged at his lips as he traced a finger over the embossed lettering of a card propped against a sleek blue box containing the black diamond bracelet he had received recently at his office. Gavin had sent them to himself, carefully choosing each item to reflect the kind of thoughtful, intimate gifts a loving husband might give. It wasn't deception—it was a rehearsal, a small indulgence to savor the feeling of being cherished by Eric. His soon-to-be husband if everything went according to plan. These moments of fantasy kept him steady, a small piece of the future he was determined to manifest.

Then, there was the memory of seeing Eric kiss Jason outside the hospital that sent a surge of anger through Gavin. *Jason.* Of course, it made sense—Jason was Eric's real husband. That instance, at the hospital, the way they embraced, had shaken him to the core. It was the first time he had actually seen the husbands intimate. But Gavin wasn't one to be deterred by inconvenient truths. He was patient. He would wait, and eventually, Jason wouldn't matter.

He thought about the music recitals, sitting in the back row of the elementary school auditorium, watching Ashton delicately play his trumpet. He had blended in perfectly. Other parents probably thought he was just another dad watching his kid perform. The lights dimmed, the music started, and there was Ashton on stage, trumpet in hand. Gavin's heart swelled with pride, even though he had no right to feel it. He wasn't really part of their lives—yet. But he would be. He just needed the right time, the right opportunity.

Ashton's birthday party had been another occasion of quiet satisfaction. Gavin remembered sitting on a park bench, far enough away not to draw attention but close enough to watch everything. He'd known about the party from the invitation he had found during one of his visits to Eric and Jason's home as a real estate agent. It was right there on the refrigerator—an open invitation, practically begging him to attend. He couldn't resist. Watching Ashton run around with his friends, laughing, playing—it felt like Gavin was observing a life that should have been his all along. A life he was sure he could step into soon enough.

As he adjusted his tie once more, Gavin's thoughts shifted to tonight. Tonight was crucial. He would meet Eric professionally, but this was more than just presenting an offer. This was his chance to make an impression and show Eric that he was the man who could be part of their lives.

Not Jason.
Not anyone else.

Just him.

Soon, Gavin thought with a smile, once Eric saw him for who he really was, he'd be invited to all those events. He wouldn't have to watch from the sidelines anymore. He would be part of their lives. He would make sure of it.

Taking one last look in the mirror, Gavin nodded at his reflection. *Perfect.* He was ready.

Chapter 26

Dr. Jacobs locked the door to his office behind him, the familiar click of the latch echoing in the narrow hallway. It had been a long, exhausting day filled with the usual assortment of troubled patients. But something about today left a nagging feeling in the pit of his stomach, a sense of apprehension that had settled there since his last conversation with Gavin.

He adjusted his coat as he stepped out onto the sidewalk, the cool evening air brushing against his skin. The city around him was alive, though quieter than usual, the sound of traffic distant and muted. Streetlights flickered to life as twilight deepened, casting pools of yellow light on the damp pavement. The subtle scent of rain lingered in the air, mixing with the faint odor of gasoline and street food from the nearby vendors.

As he walked, Dr. Jacobs couldn't shake the feeling that something was off. His pace quickened instinctively, and his mind began to race. There was no logical reason for him to be nervous—this was his usual route, the same streets he had walked hundreds of times. But tonight, the alleyways seemed darker, the shadows longer.

He glanced over his shoulder, half-expecting to see someone behind him, but the street remained empty. Still, the hairs on the back of his neck prickled, and his heartbeat quickened in his chest. He pressed forward, taking his usual shortcut through a narrow alley. It would shave a few minutes off his walk back to his apartment.

The alley was quiet, the walls on either side rising like tall, indifferent sentinels. The dim light from a distant streetlamp barely reached this far, leaving much of the passage cloaked in shadow. His footsteps echoed eerily off the walls, each step a reminder of how alone he was.

And then he saw it—a dark figure slipping out from beside a dumpster, moving quickly and deliberately toward him.

Dr. Jacobs froze, his breath catching in his throat. His heart hammered as the figure drew closer, the shadows peeling away to reveal more detail. His mind raced, trying to make sense of what was happening, but the figure lunged at him before he could react.

A sharp, sudden pain shot through his abdomen as the figure struck. His vision blurred, the world around him spinning as he staggered backward, trying to make sense of the agony radiating from his body. His hands instinctively reached for his wound, warm blood seeping through his fingers.

He gasped for breath, struggling to stay upright. And then, through the haze of pain, he saw the face of his attacker. His eyes widened in shock, recognition hitting him like a second blow.

"Gavin... why...?" Dr. Jacobs whispered, his voice weak, barely audible.

Those were the last words he would ever speak.

Gavin stood over him, his face cold and expressionless, the knife still glinting faintly in the dim light of the alley. He didn't answer. He didn't need to. Dr. Jacobs was already gone, the life draining from his body as he crumpled to the ground, blood pooling around him.

Gavin crouched down, moving with unsettling calmness. He slipped off Dr. Jacobs' expensive shoes, unclasped his designer belt, and rifled through his pockets, taking the wallet without hesitation. It had to look like a mugging—a random act of violence—something to throw off any suspicion.

Satisfied with his work, Gavin stood and glanced down at the lifeless body one last time before stepping over it, leaving the alley as quietly as he had entered. The night swallowed him up, the sound of the city fading as he disappeared into the distance.

The rain began to fall again, soft and steady, washing away the blood and the evidence of what had just transpired. The streetlights flickered, casting long shadows that danced across the alley, but no one was left to see them.

Gavin had vanished into the night and with him, any hope of redemption.

Chapter 27

The lake house was as stunning as ever, perched on the edge of the pristine waters, even after the sun had set. The trees around the property swayed gently in the breeze, their leaves rustling softly. Gavin paused, taking it all in. This was the moment he had been waiting for. Everything had led to this point. He straightened his jacket, took a deep breath, and walked toward the front door, his laptop bag slung over one shoulder, a clipboard in hand.

The sound of his footsteps on the stone path felt louder than usual, each step bringing him closer to what he knew would be an unforgettable encounter. He knocked on the heavy oak door, the cool air brushing against his face, heightening his anticipation. The lake shimmered in the distance from the reflecting moonlight, and the house seemed to breathe with an air of quiet elegance.

Shortly, the door swung open, revealing Dr. Eric Clarke standing on the threshold. He was dressed casually, his face soft with curiosity, yet his eyes held a kind of tiredness. In an instance, time seemed to stop, but Gavin kept his composure, offering his best professional smile.

"Dr. Clarke... Gavin Hayes," he introduced himself, extending his hand.

Eric smiled warmly, reaching out to shake Gavin's hand. His grip was firm but friendly. "Yes, a pleasure. We haven't formally met, but I've seen you showing the house before."

The sound of their handshake was firm but quiet, the formality between them almost palpable. Gavin nodded coolly, doing his best to hide the rush of emotions inside him. This was the first time he was truly face-to-face with Eric, and he had to play it right.

"Well, it's great to finally meet you officially," Gavin said, a bit too casually, as he adjusted the strap of his laptop bag. "I've brought everything we need for the sale and documents to sign."

Eric stepped aside, holding the door wider. "Come on in. Ashton and I were just finishing up some things around the house."

As Gavin stepped inside, the house welcomed him with its open, airy design. It felt warm and lived-in. He could imagine himself in a place like this with his new husband and son—he could see how it could all work out, just as he had planned. The hardwood floors gleamed under the light.

Just as they were heading toward the living room, a small figure bounded into the room. Ashton, with his bright eyes and curious smile, appeared. The instant Gavin saw him, his heart skipped a beat, and his face lit up.

"Ashton!" Gavin said, his voice enthusiastic but warm. "It's good to see you!" He slipped his hand into his laptop bag and pulled out a small, colorful toy—one of the Hunchkins figurines he had bought weeks ago. "I actually brought something for you. I happened to notice your Hunchkin figurine collection upstairs when I was giving tours, and I thought you might like this."

Ashton's eyes widened with excitement as Gavin handed him the figurine. It was bright turquoise with the long ears of a rabbit but the plump body and curly tail of a pig, its little snout speckled with light pink freckles. The Hunchkin wore a miniature yellow bandana around its neck, and its wide, round eyes sparkled. It was a playful, goofy little toy—just the kind of thing a child Ashton's age would adore.

"You bet Ashton loves Hunchkins," Eric said, beaming as he watched his son.

Ashton took the toy, his face lighting up with pure joy. "Thank you!" he exclaimed, looking up at Gavin with bright, grateful eyes.

Eric smiled proudly, giving Gavin an approving look. There was a slight twinkle in his eye, one that caught Gavin off guard, as if the gesture had meant more to Eric than Gavin expected.

"You're very welcome," Gavin said, his voice softening as Ashton turned and ran off. The sound of his footsteps echoed through the hall as he went to play with his new toy and add it to his collection.

Gavin watched the boy go, his heart swelling with a strange sense of fulfillment. He could feel Eric's gaze still on him and turned to meet it. Their eyes locked, and Gavin felt the intensity of that exact second—the recognition of something unspoken, something he couldn't quite name.

"You're really good with him," Eric said after a pause, his voice genuine.

Gavin shrugged modestly, though his heart was racing. "He's a great kid. And... well, I guess I just wanted to do something special for him after all he's been through recently."

Eric nodded, his smile lingering a bit longer before he gestured toward the kitchen island. "Let's go ahead and take a seat. We can go over the offer, and I'll sign whatever you need."

As Gavin followed Eric into the kitchen, he couldn't help but feel that things were falling into place, just as he had envisioned. The connection was forming; the pieces of his plan were clicking together. All that was left to do was to keep moving forward, one step at a time.

And tonight, he would take that next step.

The kitchen of the lake house was as pristine and elegant as the rest of the home. The vast quartz island stretched out in front of them, gleaming under the soft glow of the overhead lights.

Gavin set his laptop bag on the island, carefully removing the sleek silver device and his clipboard. He opened the laptop with practiced ease, turning it to face Eric as he pulled out the necessary paperwork from the clipboard. His movements were smooth and calm, though, beneath the surface, a rush of anticipation coursed through him. This was it—the culmination of everything he had planned.

"Now," Gavin said, offering Eric a warm, professional smile. "Let me show you what I brought for you."

They stood side by side at the island, and Gavin couldn't help but steal glances at Eric as he set the papers down. Eric looked tired—understandably so—but there was a quiet strength in how he carried himself. His strong and defined jawline caught the light just right, and his slightly tousled dark hair only added to his casual, effortless appeal. Gavin's eyes drifted down the length of Eric's frame, lingering on the slight creases of his button-down shirt and the way his hands rested on the edge of the countertop, steady but gentle. Every detail about him seemed to radiate an understated beauty.

Eric looked over the paperwork Gavin laid out in front of him, his brow furrowing slightly as he scanned the documents. "Please, read over the offer," Gavin said, his voice steady. "I think it's a really good one. Just contact Spencer or me if you have any immediate questions. The buyer does expect to have an answer in the next twenty-four hours."

Eric let out a deep sigh, his eyes glancing over the numbers. His fingers lightly traced the edges of the paper, and Gavin couldn't help but admire the way his hands moved and how composed he was, even in a moment like this. As Eric scanned the documents, Gavin studied him intently, captivated by every detail—his expression, the way his lips pressed together in thought, the soft rise and fall of his chest as he breathed.

After a brevity of silence, Eric glanced up, meeting Gavin's gaze briefly before looking back down at the papers. "It's really a good price. Just what we asked for. Yeah," he said softly. "I'm sure we can make this work."

Gavin nodded, a slight smile tugging at the corner of his lips. "My clients will be very pleased."

A long pause followed, the quiet between them filled only by the soft hum of the refrigerator and the distant sound of Ashton playing in another room. Eric's gaze wandered around the kitchen, his eyes moving from the walls to the windows, taking in every inch of the home.

"This place..." Eric started, his voice quieter now. "My husband and I... we were really happy here."

There was a deep sadness in his voice, a weight that hung in the air. Gavin felt a pang of sympathy in his chest, but he quickly pushed it aside, keeping his expression calm and measured. "I heard about what happened," Gavin said gently, his voice softening. "You have my deepest condolences."

Eric nodded, his eyes distant as if he were looking back through time, through memories. "Thank you," he replied. He glanced back at Gavin, his face marked with that same tiredness but also a quiet resolve. "We... Ashton and I... we planned on moving downtown to shorten my commute. That way, I can spend more time with him. My family. I guess that's more important now than ever, isn't it?"

Gavin swallowed hard, his throat tightening just slightly as he nodded. "Yes," he said softly, his voice thick with meaning. "Family is the most important thing in the world."

About the Author

B.J. Irons works in the field of education as a college professor and educational leader. Many of his personal experiences as a gay man have contributed to his books. Being a part of the LGBTQIA+ community himself, B.J. hopes to continue to bring more colorful and fun fictional works to his LGBTQIA+ readers.

Excellent LGBTQ+ fiction by unique, wonderful authors.

Thrillers

Mystery

Romance

Literary

Young Adult

& More

Join our mailing list for new, offers, and free books!

Visit our website for more Spectrum Books

www.spectrum-books.com

Or find us on Instagram @spectrumbookpublisher

www.ingramcontent.com/pod-product-compliance
Lightning Source LLC
Chambersburg PA
CBHW011957090526
44590CB00023B/3759